Law

and

Psychology

in

Conflict

By JAMES MARSHALL

THE BOBBS-MERRILL COMPANY, INC.
A subsidiary of Howard W. Sams & Co., Inc
Publishers • INDIANAPOLIS • KANSAS CITY • NEW YORK

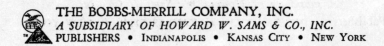
THE BOBBS-MERRILL COMPANY, INC.
A SUBSIDIARY OF HOWARD W. SAMS & CO., INC.
PUBLISHERS • INDIANAPOLIS • KANSAS CITY • NEW YORK

To my grandchildren, with
love and the hope that they
will search for and face reality.

FOREWORD

Man's ability to think depends almost wholly on his ability to observe and recall what he has observed. Logic is a futile and arid exercise without data. But we have no data save by the evidence of our senses. So the reliability of evidence provided by human senses is fundamental to rational thought.

It is no new discovery that our senses often mislead us and that the data provided by observation and recall are often in error. Since antiquity men have been conscious of deficiencies in their data, although only the most thoughtful were aware of the extent of these deficiencies. In the Seventh Book of Plato's *Republic*, Socrates likens human beings to prisoners living in an underground den who have been chained since childhood so they cannot move or turn their heads and who can see only the wall of the cave. The cave has a mouth open toward the light and a fire is blazing at a distance. Between the fire and the prisoners there is a path along which men pass, carrying all sorts of vessels and statues and figures made of various materials. The prisoners see only the shadows which the fire throws on the opposite wall of the cave. To them the truth is literally nothing but the shadows of images. Then, Socrates continues in the dialogue, see what would follow if the prisoners were released and disabused of their error. When first liberated and compelled to turn around and look toward the light one would suffer sharp pains; the glare would distress him; and he would be unable to see the realities of which in his former state he had seen the shadows. If someone would say to him that what he saw before was an illusion but that now when his eye is turned toward more real existence he has a clearer vision, he will fancy that the shadows which he formerly saw are truer than the objects which are now shown to him. And if he is compelled to look straight at the light, he will have a pain in his eyes which will make him turn away to take refuge in the objects of vision which he can see, and which he will conceive to be in reality clearer than the things which are now being shown to him.

Although the author of this book does not invoke the Platonic metaphor, the message of this book is that our courts are in the position of the prisoners of the cave. As I have pointed out elsewhere,[1] law suits are never decided on the facts since only evidence is available to the courts and this is simply a secondary indication of the facts.

In this book, Mr. Marshall shows us how the courts, both judges and juries, are like Plato's prisoners of the cave in that they watch the shadows on the wall and discuss with one another what the "reality" of the shadow is. The main burden of this book is to show that there is now a substantial body of scientific information to establish the lack of correspondence between the shadows on the wall (or the testimony in court) and the actual figures passing before the opening of the cave (that is, the events with which the law suit is concerned). The data of experimental psychology now establish quite securely that no two individuals observe any complex occurrence in quite the same manner; that the ability of different individuals to retain and recall observations differs; that the elements which are retained and recalled are influenced by past experience and attitudes; and that the ability of various individuals to express what they have observed, retained and recalled varies greatly. There is no wholly reliable witness since the observation of all witnesses is faulty in some degree and some situations.

In the intellectual history of mankind, the two principal methods developed for securing and testing data have been scientific research and the adversary trial. By and large these have been used in different situations and have different purposes. For reasons that are not very readily apparent, the fact-finding processes of science and of law have had relatively little effect upon one another. The message that Mr. Marshall brings in this book is that this condition cannot continue. He gathers here the results of most of the scientific work that has been done in the field of evidentiary reliability and includes a report of an interesting original experiment of his own in this area. The conclusion which he reaches is that the scientific data now known make "acute the need for a complete reconsideration of the rules of evidence to conform them overall instead of piecemeal to what we know of the human condition." Few scholars of the law of evidence will quarrel with this conclusion. But more than the scholars should be concerned. Lawyers, legislators and informed citizens should be aware of the problems inherent

---

[1] Loevinger, *Facts, Evidence and Legal Proof*, 9 W. RES. L. REV. 154 (1958); HENSON, LANDMARKS OF LAW 422 (1960).

in the investigation of facts by human testimony. This volume not only makes it possible for everyone to gain this insight but also makes it an interesting, and even exciting, intellectual experience. No attempt is made here to present any authoritative or official answers, for none are yet available to most of the problems examined. What the author does do is to present the questions and problems that must be considered if law is to continue to perform its central function in our society.

There will, no doubt, be lawyers and judges who will react to material in this book as Plato's prisoners of the cave reacted to the sunlight and the sight of the world of solid objects which they had previously seen only by shadow. Some will insist that we must rely on testimony and that, since we do not know the precise limits of its accuracy, we should ignore its defects and limitations. As Plato observed so long ago, to those accustomed to darkness the light is painful, to those accustomed to shadows solid objects are unreal. But light has the power to dispel darkness and shadows are no match for solid objects. There is no choice in this matter. We may ignore reality but we cannot escape it. This book is an effort to help us face the ubiquitous problem of making evidence correspond with facts. This is a challenge to all who are concerned with the processes of law. It is also the first task of any man who would be rational in his approach to the world.

Lee Loevinger

ACKNOWLEDGEMENTS

The Author gratefully acknowledges the assistance of the following:

The late Professor Arthur R. Cohen, who was helpful in discussing the plan of this book; Professors Hadley Cantril and Marc Franklin, for their advice; Mrs. Ruth Franklin, for her research help; his partner, Morton S. Robson, for his suggestions; and Mrs. Miriam S. Frank and Mrs. Arlene Polsky Jones, for the difficult job of typing and arranging the book.

In connection with research in Chapter II, the Author is indebted to Dr. Helge Mansson, who conducted the experiments reported jointly with the Author, and John Van-Esen, for his careful and laborious technical help; to Professor Isidor Chein, for his advice; to Professors Henry H. Foster, Jr. and Gerhardt Mueller, for advising and participating in the law school experiment, Miss Helen Hall and Mr. Felipe Ortez, for help in the experiment at the Henry Street Settlement, Chief Deputy Inspector George P. McManus and Captains Vincent T. Agoglis and Joseph A. Preiss, in connection with the experiment at the New York Police Academy; to Miss Keitha Tompkins, for rating answers to the questionnaires; and the National Broadcasting Company and Lawrence K. Grossman, of N.B.C., for the film used.

CONTENTS

CHAPTER III. IN THE COURTROOM

ILLUSTRATIONS

INTRODUCTION

Explaining his difficulties with the evidence on which he based his conclusions, Thucydides talked of "the want of coincidence between accounts of the same occurrences by different eyewitnesses, arising sometimes from imperfect memory, sometimes from undue partiality for one side or the other." Of the speeches which he reported, some of which he had himself heard, some of which he had heard from others, he wrote that "It was in all cases difficult to carry them word for word in one's memory, so my habit has been to make the speakers say what was in my opinion demanded of them by the various occasions, of course adhering as closely as possible to the general sense of what they really said." [1]

Thucydides' difficulty in discerning the realities of events from eyewitnesses and those who had heard relevant statements plagues the law of evidence today. His experiences with the problem of arriving at reality from his own and others' memories have been validated by the findings of modern psychology. The very perceptions on which recollection is founded tend to be inaccurate, for they reflect not so much the objective qualities of what has been seen and heard as the expectations or preconceptions that the observer brings to the event and his "transactions" or interactions with others who may have been involved.

For the law, the basic problem of truth does not arise so much from the villainy of perjurers and suborners of perjury as from the unreliability of personal observation. As Shaw said in his "Introduction" to *Saint Joan*, "It is what men do at their best, with good intentions, and what normal men and women find that they must and will do in spite of their intentions, that really concern us." [2]

We are the heirs of the Natural Law philosophers and the theologians who polarized everything as good and bad, right and wrong, whereas the very nature of science on

---

[1] THUCYDIDES, COMPLETE WRITINGS 14 (Modern Library ed. Crawley transl. 1951).

[2] SHAW, SAINT JOAN 51 (Modern Library ed. 1956).

which our industrial society is based is that conclusions are *always* conditional — conditioned by time, place, situation, observer, as well as by the possibility that new evidence may result in new conclusions.[3] From laboratory experiment we are informed: "Actually . . . cleverness, or worth themselves are largely a function of *who makes the statements and to whom they are made.*"[4]

This tendency to polarize originates in our early acculturation. In childhood we relate to members of the family and learn that we must "be on one side or the other."[5]

We are inclined to accept those who accept us and reject those who reject us,[6] and, similarly, to accept the ideas of those who accept us, *i.e.*, the "good" people, and reject the ideas of those who reject us, *i.e.*, the "bad" people. For example, we tend to believe the man who hits us is in the wrong; and the man we hit did the wrong thing, not we. He is the "bad" one. It was the other fellow who drove negligently and was responsible for the accident. ". . . This tendency to regress to simple categories of perception is especially strong under conditions of emotional stress and external threat. Witness our readiness in times of war to exalt the virtues of our own side and to see the enemy as thoroughly evil."[7] On the other hand, as George Eliot said in *Middlemarch,* "The text, whether of prophet or poet, expands for whatever we can put into it, and even his bad grammar is sublime."

Hugo Münsterberg, who dramatized in his classes the inaccuracies of observation of events occurring in the room, was one of the first scholars to point out the discrepancies between evidence of the senses and evidence of the law. Although social-psychology has developed and modified many of his ideas, his genius stands out in its application of experimental psychology to the courtroom. In his *On the Witness Stand,* first published in 1908, he described discrepancies between perception and recall as psychological

---

[3] Lundberg, *Conflicting Orientation in Law and National Policy,* in TAYLOR, LIFE, LANGUAGE, LAW 168 (1957).

[4] Horwitz, Lyons & Perlmutter, *Induction of Forces in Discussion Groups,* 4, No. 1 HUMAN RELATIONS 57, 74 (1951).

[5] SAUL, THE HOSTILE MIND 130-31 (1956).

[6] Brown, *Models of Attitude Change,* in BROWN, GALANTIER, HESS & MANDLER, 1 NEW DIRECTIONS IN PSYCHOLOGY 38-39 (1962).

[7] Bronfenbrenner, *The Mirror Image in Soviet-American Relations, A Social Psychologist's Report,* 17, No. 3 J. SOCIAL ISSUES 45-56 (1961).

processes and the assumptions of the courtroom regarding them. He also pointed out some of the deficiencies in trial procedure from the viewpoint of psychology.[8] Some of his experiments are well known. They are repeated in classrooms and frequently referred to by lawyers. Their validity has not been questioned, but their application to the law has not been attempted. It is as though lawyers admitted the contradiction between psychology and traditional legal practices and held up their hands in despair at the thought of experimenting to eliminate them, to make possible testimony that is more reliable.

In the 1920's, in the course of an intellectual quest for a truth that could be discovered experientially, some consideration was given to the relationship between psychological findings and the rules of evidence. A few studies were presented as observations on the laws of evidence under the auspices of Robert Hutchins and Donald Slesinger at Yale and Mortimer Adler and Jerome Michael at Columbia, but these were essentially exploratory. "By careful use of [the scientists'] . . . proved results in these and other fields," Hutchins and Slesinger wrote, "we may yet build a law of evidence more closely related to the facts of human behavior." [9]

It is the purpose of this book to carry this line of thought further in the light of more recent studies by social-psychologists. First will be considered the conflict between the law of evidence and empirical research and the need to press further research to devise means to gain greater accuracy in evidence on which to determine responsibility, damages, and guilt. Secondly, there will be discussion of the trial process and its effects on the search for reality.

---

[8] MÜNSTERBERG, ON THE WITNESS STAND: ESSAYS ON PSYCHOLOGY AND CRIME 15-36, 50 (1923) and PSYCHOLOGY: GENERAL AND APPLIED ch. 30 (1915).

[9] Hutchins & Slesinger, *Some Observations on the Law of Evidence —Memory*, 41 HARV. L. REV. 860, 873 (1928).

CHAPTER I

PSYCHOLOGY AND EVIDENCE

I. The Setting

The atmosphere of the courtroom is not normally such that one could expect to find the truth of a situation; at best one finds only a rough approximation. The courtroom is not a laboratory. As one lawyer addressing others concluded: "I don't have to tell you that a law suit is not a disinterested investigation but a bitter adversary duel." [10]

Francis Wellman, speaking of cross-examination, says: "It is a mental duel between counsel and witness." [11] He continues: "It is the love of combat which every man possesses that fastens the attention of the jury upon the progress of the trial." [12] He might have added that most cases are so dull in their succession of witnesses and documents that only the element of combat they contain can hold the attention of judge and jury.

In important cases the impartial objectives of the courtroom are further contaminated by the public drama stimulated by the mass media. The famous *Hall-Mills* case was full of testimony from witnesses whose perception and knowledge of the case was evidently stimulated by the newspaper accounts and the notoriety involved.[13]

The moves and counter-moves of attorneys "pursuant to a complex system of rules, each trying to gain advantage for its cause," and the stimulant of publicity which affected court and counsel, are revealed by the story of the trial of Jack Ruby. Ruby killed Oswald, the assassin of Presi-

---

[10] Gair, *The Dynamics of a Negligence Trial*, 19 N.Y. COUNTY LAW. A.B. BULL. 110, 114 (1962).

[11] WELLMAN, THE ART OF CROSS-EXAMINATION 8 (1936).

[12] *Id.* at 14.

[13] KUNSTLER, THE MINISTER AND THE CHOIR SINGER (1964).

dent Kennedy, while an estimated sixty million watched
at their television sets. In the Ruby trial everything was
distorted and almost every distortion was in full view of
millions of people.[13a]

Although it is a crime to tamper with the jury, jurors
are under constant pressure from newspapers, television,
and radio, which prejudge the case or at least the witnesses.
From these sources, jurors may receive documents and testimony excluded by the judge. At a trial of Billy Sol Estes
in Texas, his lawyers, during the impaneling of the jury,
said that the only acceptable venireman was one of Latin-
American origin who could neither read nor write, the assumption being that the others had already been exposed
to too much prejudicial material in the press. The British
are more realistic and prohibit such interference by the
mass media.

Dean Wigmore would have us distinguish between " 'contentiousness,' which is a fault of behavior, and 'contentious
procedure,' which merely denotes the scientific fact that
our system relies upon *the parties, not the judge,* to search
for evidence and to present it, each in rivalry with the
other. The former may be merely a remediable abuse,
separable from the system itself; the latter may be a sound
principle." [14] The question arises as to the criteria by which
soundness is measured. Is a field dominated by hostility,
for example, one in which objective data can reasonably
be procured?

At times, seemingly respectable attorneys will, to win
a case, indulge in trickery though it may mean the very
life of a defendant. A dramatic example of this occurred
in the cross-examination of a witness and the summation
by the assistant district attorney in the celebrated murder
trial of Nan Patterson.[15] Clever cross-examination intended
as a means to justice became an end in itself and the
"mental duel" became a self-sufficing exercise though the
executioner awaited the conclusion.

This courtroom combat, this "adversary duel," is a
sublimation of more direct forms of hostile aggression in

[13a] KAPLAN & WALTZ, THE TRIAL OF JACK RUBY 9 (1965).

[14] 1 WIGMORE, EVIDENCE § 8c, at 284-85 (3d ed. 1940).

[15] LEVY, THE NAN PATTERSON CASE ch. 24 (1959); and see examples of legitimatized tricks of the trade by the district attorney in
the trial of Jack Ruby, KAPLAN & WALTZ, *op. cit. supra* note 13, at
106-08, 155.

primitive societies, such as blood feuds and individual or clan acts of revenge. It is a game we play within rules called laws of jurisdiction and of evidence, laws criminal and civil. As a sublimation of direct action this serves a useful social purpose, for the element of competition and the release of hostility are essential. But the combat, the duel, the game are certainly not the best ways to discover truth, nor are they well calculated to arrive at just compensation or fitting penalties.

Seeking the truth, fact, or reality in this unscientific atmosphere, the court hears evidence. We are not so much concerned here with the rules of evidence themselves as with the quality or value of the evidence offered under the rules. Indeed, the artificiality of many of the rules of evidence has led to an excessive focus on the means at the expense of the end. Dean Wigmore notes that the rules have become more rationalized in theory but less rationally applied toward "the ascertainment of truth . . . fought over with irrelevant snarling and yapping." [16]

Nor are we primarily concerned with the problem of perjured testimony. When there is a conflict in evidence the court attempts to discover which side is telling the truth, whereas frequently the question is: Is either side telling the truth? For "evidence itself is far less trustworthy than the public usually realizes. . . . People as a rule do not reflect upon their meager opportunities for observing facts, and rarely suspect the frailty of their own powers of observation. They come to court, if summoned as witnesses, prepared to tell what they think they know; and in the beginning they resent an attack upon their story as they would upon their integrity." [17]

Mr. Justice Cardozo suggests that "As political economy has its economic man, so jurisprudence has its reasonable man, its negligent man," etc. The law, he tells us, "is no stranger to the philosophy of the 'As If.' It has built up many of its doctrines by make-believe that things are other than they are." [18]

---

[16] Wigmore, *Jury-Trial Rules of Evidence in the Next Century*, in LAW: A CENTURY OF PROGRESS 1835-1935, at 347 (Reppy ed. 1937).

[17] WELLMAN, *op. cit. supra* note 11, at 7, 10.

[18] CARDOZO, THE PARADOXES OF LEGAL SCIENCE 33-34 (1928), referring to VAIHINGER, DIE PHILOSOPHIE DES ALS OB [THE PHILOSOPHY OF THE "AS IF"] (Ogden transl. 1935).

Because law has not developed its own experimental discipline, it has the responsibility to test its "make-believe" doctrine by whatever scientific methods are available and adjust those doctrines insofar as it can to reality. If the law cannot achieve this within the traditions of the courtroom, then it would seem that substitute legal institutions should be provided whenever they are better suited to reality. Whenever the "As If" can be replaced by the "Is," the make-believe should give way.

II. The Make-Believe of Evidence

Let us take a look at some of the principal "As Ifs" related to evidence. Except in commercial cases, the greater part of evidence introduced into the courts is testimony of what the eyewitness saw, what the hearer heard and what the witness remembers of occurrences, sometimes occurrences years distant in time. Implicit, if not always explicit, is the assumption that witnesses can see accurately, hear accurately, and recall accurately. This assumption which is the keystone "As If" of the law of evidence, is in fact contradicted by the findings of psychological science.

There are many points between the occurrence and the verdict at which the incident in dispute may be distorted, intentionally or not. The areas in which the witness might unwittingly distort that which happens may be divided into three categories: [19] (A) *Perception,* including (1) the limitations on the range and acuteness of human sense perception and (2) the way events are interpreted and significances assigned to them (*i.e.,* the determination of sense perception) by a person's idiosyncratic needs, moods, and emotions; (B) *Recollection,* the time lapse between the accident and its recounting, during which other influences on the observer permit the image of the incident to be altered;

[19] Compare Thomas, *Cross-Examination of Witnesses*, in TORT AND MEDICAL YEARBOOK 57, 72 (Averbach & Belli ed. 1961).

and (C) *Articulation,* the basic problem of communication, whereby the same words are used with different meanings by different persons. This indication of the imperfections in testimony of events concerns the refractions of the truth that relate to the witness vis-á-vis the event; comparable distortions occur during the transaction between the witness and the jurors, and among the jurors when they convene to discuss the testimony in the jury room.

A. PERCEPTION

1. RANGE AND ACUTENESS.

Modern social science has learned much about each of these areas, and especially in the category of sense perception psychologists stress the disparity between even the simplest stimulus, *i.e.,* object or event, and the perception of it. "[T]here are no concrete absolutes in perception: instead, what is perceived may roughly be described as a series of functional probabilities." [20] "Apparently," notes Kilpatrick, "the correspondence between percept and object is never absolute. Instead, perception is of functional probabilities, of constructs which emerge from the consequences of past action and serve as directives for furthering the purposes of the organism through action. 'Percept' and 'object' are but two abstracted aspects of this total process and correspondence between the two is simply a function of their being part and parcel of the same thing." [21]

What this means to the layman is that all of the physical aspects of our environment vary to each individual in terms of his own experiences. What you and I see when two cars proceed down a street and collide is not the identical cars, streets, and collisions, but cars, streets, and collisions fashioned from our respective experiences with them. Take another example. We see a young woman with two small children and, based on experience and probability, we assume she is their mother. If we have some question about our judgment we look for a wedding ring or try to hear their conversation to reinforce our conclusion.

---

[20] Kilpatrick & Cantril, *The Constancies in Social Perception,* in EXPLORATIONS IN TRANSACTIONAL PSYCHOLOGY 354-65, at 357 (Kilpatrick ed. 1961).

[21] *Id.* at 4.

Psychology views the individual, his surroundings, his past, and his future, as integrated into a continuous flow of data back and forth, through experience and through stimuli to the senses. It treats perception itself as the individual's awareness of a "thing" or "happening" conditioned by his similar experiences in the past and designed to direct his behavior in the future to be consistent with what he already knows. To these "things" or "happenings" one assigns out of his arsenal of experience significances, meanings, and values.

It is the premise of the transactional psychologists that man's basic drive is toward security, not only in the emotional sense but in terms of being in harmony with his environment. The greater the constancy of that environment, the higher the degree of security that it will yield. Change of environment requires a re-evaluation of the external world so that the individual, trying to regain his security, can realign himself with those persons or things or happenings external to him. Man's perceptions are guided by this need to maintain psychological equilibrium. To insure a predictable environment, perception can magnify or diminish the importance of certain information, and actually distort quality and size.[22]

Some simple demonstrations of how our sense perceptions are governed by what we already know about the world around us have been produced by artificially manipulating "cues" to perceptions such as size, distance, brightness, and other physical properties. Such perceptions are commonly involved in negligence cases and frequently in other litigation. It may be startling to many of us to learn that a cue to a perception of distance, for example, is a witness's prior experience with the size of objects in the field of vision. An experiment indicating this involves showing playing cards of different sizes to an observer in a darkened room where he has no points of reference for what he sees. When an observer sees, in these circumstances, a playing card that is twice the size of the conventional playing card with which his past experience has familiarized him, he is so conditioned by that past experience that he expects the card to be of the same size as those to which he is accustomed. He therefore will assume that it is in fact twice as close, rather than that it is twice

---

[22] Stagner, *Personality Dynamics and Social Conflict*, 17, No. 3 J. SOCIAL ISSUES 28, 33 (1961).

as large. These demonstrations[23] have convinced research-
ers that the perception of *where* a thing is depends on
perception of *what* a thing is and on *when* it is perceived.

Thus, in even the simplest perceptual process, the mind
takes over and adjusts what the senses report to the past
perceptual experience in order to maintain that stability
of environment on which the human organism flourishes.
Similar experiments with cigarette packs, magazines, and
other objects of standard size have reinforced this finding
that size and distance are experientially related, and that size
is the dominant "cue" that will govern the readjustment of
the perception of other characteristics. The strength of size
as a cue has been reinforced by its constancy within experience, for size is a more constant attribute of the object
itself, and less subject to variation than other perceived
characteristics such as distance, brightness, color, and consistency. A further demonstration of the role of experience
in governing these perceptions is reported by Ames and
Ittelson, who found that in the experiment with playing
cards of various sizes, only young observers, presumably
less rigidly conditioned by past experience because such
experience was more limited, could accommodate to changes
in the size of the cards.[24]

When we do not have experiential information about
size, we deduce size from whatever other strong cues are
available. A common example is the "moon illusion." The
moon looks larger on the horizon than at the zenith because
on the horizon it is seen in relation to things on the land-
scape. It is measured against things of known size at dis-
tances which we have experienced. This is not so when
the moon is "a disembodied body" overhead.[25] Rock and
Kaufman include a picture showing a black rectangle in
the foreground and another, of the same size, on the horizon.
The effect of distance on size is such that the rectangle on
the horizon seems larger than the other, although they are
exactly the same in size. This effect is greatly increased
with a three-dimensional scene where the impression of
depth is stronger. The reason for this is that the related
stimuli "that normally accompany changes in distance may

---

[23] Kilpatrick & Cantril, *op. cit. supra* note 20, at 36.
[24] See Ames, Jr. & Ittelson, *Accommodation, Convergence, and
Apparent Distance*, in EXPLORATIONS IN TRANSACTIONAL PSYCHOLOGY
99, 118 (Kilpatrick ed. 1961).
[25] Kaufman & Rock, *The Moon Illusion*, 136, No. 3521 SCIENCE 1023.

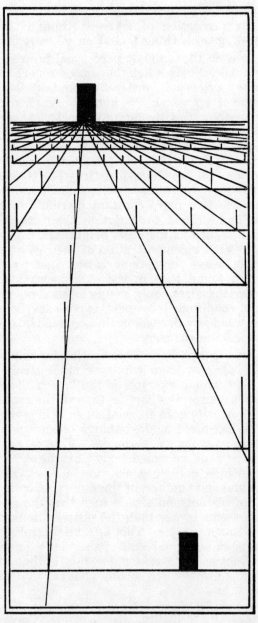

THE MOON ILLUSION

Reproduced by permission from Science Magazine.

be registered by the brain and automatically affect size perception without conscious recognition of this effect on the part of the observer." [26]

These scientific explorations of the most elementary perceptions have been carried from the laboratory test situation to the more sophisticated occurrences of daily life, and applied to *aural* as well as visual perception.[27] Witnesses testify to what they heard as well as to what they saw. What do they hear? Kilpatrick reports that the novel sound of an oncoming tornado was conformed to past experience by many hearers who accepted it as the sound of an oncoming train; thus perceptual similarities are converted by the observer into identities in order to maintain the stability of his environment and thus his harmony with it.

As Thucydides suggested, we do something very similar when we *recall* spoken words. We reconstruct conversations "of course adhering as closely as possible to the general sense of what was really said." [28] None of us hears all the words or other sounds that occur in our presence. Many of us are deaf to certain tones and we miss the words or syllables in that tonal range, or we have some other diminution in hearing. What we do to adjust to such phenomena in normal conversation, or in listening to lecturers or arguments, is to fill in blanks as we believe the speaker might have meant them. We put together what we have heard with what we sense we might have missed in order to make a whole which is acceptable to us, thereby conforming our perceptions to our expectations. Obviously, this provides an opportunity to realize our expectations, to engage in wishful thinking. Thus a witness can in good honor swear to the truth of what he did not hear, to a damaging statement which a party never made or perhaps made in terms that were in reality not damaging to him.

It is difficult to resist the temptation at times to cite fiction rather than research to illustrate psychological phenomena. The author cannot resist referring to the song of Alice's friend the Knight when she went *Through the Looking Glass* to illustrate selective listening. The Knight described questioning an aged, aged man "A-sitting on a

---

[26] *Id.* No. 3520, at 961 n.1.

[27] Kilpatrick, *Perception in Critical Situations*, in Explorations in Transactional Psychology 316-20 (Kilpatrick ed. 1961).

[28] Thucydides, Complete Writings, *op. cit. supra* note 1.

gate" concerning his age and how he lived. The aged man
made several attempts to answer, but the Knight admitted:

> ". . . his answer trickled through my head
> Like water through a sieve."

The Knight meanwhile was thinking of other things, until
the aged, aged man ended by saying:

> "And very gladly will I drink
> To your Honor's noble health."

This last point made a pleasing impression on the Knight.[29]
He could hear it. When we ask questions, frequently we
don't listen to the answer, except when it is something
that we want to hear, something that gives us support.

This selective process and inventive reconstruction of
conversations has been recognized in law by "the hearsay
rule." The law has long attempted to avoid testimony of
hearsay that cannot be balanced by rebuttal. But even
when the testimony of a witness can be modified or refuted
by another witness, both reports are inevitably selective
and inventive. Rumor is a form of hearsay and as such
is not admitted in evidence (except in such instances as
character testimony) because the law recognizes that it is
imprecise, selective, and secondhand. Rumor does, however,
affect the processes of perception and recall because it is an
experience. For, by the process already described, in order
to maintain harmony with his environment, one who hears a
rumor will often tend to accredit it to his own perception.

The gap created by a lack of knowledge or perception,
of some fact that we deem necessary to reach a conclusion,
will tend to create in us a sense of incongruity with respect
to the remaining data. Therefore, in order to dispel this
incongruity, we try to fill the gap by obtaining further
data. But the jury cannot do this once they are in the jury
room, except perhaps by having a portion of the testimony
read to them. This, however, may not meet their needs.
What happens then is what happens frequently in other
situations. The gap may be filled in with rumor. Frequently
this gap in knowledge arouses suspicion and jurymen may
create their own rumor or even gossip. This rumor can
be of such a character as will justify some fear or stress

[29] CARROLL, ALICE'S ADVENTURES IN WONDERLAND and THROUGH
THE LOOKING GLASS 177, 180 (Macmillan & Co. ed. 1930).

that the jurors may have. It may act to justify either hostile or affirmative feelings they have against one of the parties, witnesses, or attorneys.[30]

We sometimes read drama into perception. For example, when two moving dots are shown on a screen, the larger behind the smaller, the larger is perceived as "chasing" the smaller. But when the larger is shown in front, it is generally seen as "leading." [31] The perception reflects some of our earliest childhood experiences. What we define as "good" or "bad" reflects in our perception of such matters as the facial expression of men on a picket line. To the management it appears "threatening," to labor "determined."[32]

An automobile accident is an exceedingly complex and sudden occurrence taking less than ten seconds.[33] No matter how accurately it is observed, it cannot be perceived in an exact manner by any witness. In other words, not only is eyewitness testimony of such an occurrence necessarily inaccurate; it is also in essential points incomplete.

In many tort and criminal cases *duration of events* is an important factor. Witnesses are asked to testify as to the interval between an occurrence and the action of a party or some third person. Experiments have demonstrated that we do not judge the passage of time accurately, and that "visual durations that were the same as auditory durations were judged shorter," [34] by about twenty percent.[35]

Danger and stress also affect the estimate of time and distance. This overestimate tends to increase as danger increases. As laymen we are accustomed to the concept that in emergencies time seems endless, but as lawyers we ignore the reality that with increasing danger "space and time stretch," [36] and so accept the validity of a party's testimony that the car was a hundred yards away when he

[30] FESTINGER, A THEORY OF COGNITIVE DISSONANCE 235-43 (1957).

[31] Heider & Simmel, *An Experimental Study of Apparent Behavior*, 57 AMERICAN J. PSYCHOLOGY 243, 254 (1944).

[32] OSGOOD, GRADUATED RECIPROCATION IN TENSION-REDUCTION 22 (n.d.).

[33] NORMAN, ROAD TRAFFIC ACCIDENTS (1962).

[34] Goldstone, Bordman & Lhamon, *Intersensory Comparisons of Temporal Judgments*, 57 J. EXPERIMENTAL PSYCHOLOGY 243-48 (1959).

[35] Behar & Bevar, *The Perceived Duration of Auditory and Visual Intervals: Cross Model Comparison and Interaction*, 74 AMERICAN J. PSYCHOLOGY 17-26 (1961).

[36] Langer, Wapner & Werner, *The Effect of Danger Upon the Experience of Time*, 74 AMERICAN J. PSYCHOLOGY 94-97 (1961).

stepped off the curb, or the statement of a car driver as
to when he sounded his horn. Not only the duration, but
the *sequence* of events may be difficult to perceive. This
too may be an important issue of fact, as when the question
in an assault case is who struck first, or in a matrimonial
proceeding, who spoke first.[37]

The law of evidence takes a contrary view concerning
the impact of stress. The *res gestae* rule governing the
admission of spontaneous explanations by a participant
in an event is justified on the theory that the impact of
intensity, the "stress of nervous excitement" as Dean Wigmore calls it, will make for "a spontaneous and sincere
response. . . ." [38] That is, legal theory maintains that in the
"stress of nervous excitement" the witness does not consciously try to make self-serving declarations as to his perceptions, and therefore his statements are more reliable. It
ignores, however, the distorting impact of trauma on the
capacity to perceive.

The importance of judging distance when observing an
automobile accident is obvious. Yet if *distance perception*
is merely a secondary or derivative perception, as has been
shown, then any witness's report of distance must be subject to so many other conditions that it may be unreliable.
Another essential of any eyewitness report of an automobile
accident is perception of motion, and this too has been
demonstrated to be a secondary, or derivative, characteristic, dependent upon size, apparent distance, lighting, angle
of vision, and the known attributes of the object perceived
in motion.[39]

With respect to relative size, Gardner notes that we
tend to overestimate the length of verticals, and to exaggerate the difference if one average-sized person is sur-
rounded by many exceptionally short or tall ones, and find
that the one person is the exception and the others are the
average.[40]

---

[37] Doehring, *Accuracy and Consistency of Time-Estimation by Four
Methods of Reproduction*, 74 AMERICAN J. PSYCHOLOGY 27 et seq.
(1961) (describing experiments on individual's ability to judge time);
and see ch. II.

[38] 6 WIGMORE, EVIDENCE § 1747, at 135 (3d ed. 1940).

[39] Kilpatrick & Ittelson, *The Perception of Movement*, in EXPLORA-
TIONS IN TRANSACTIONAL PSYCHOLOGY 58-68 (Kilpatrick ed. 1961).

[40] Gardner, *The Perception and Memory of Witnesses*, 18 CORNELL
L.Q. 391-98 (1933).

In view of the frequent use of *photographs*, a word about them is relevant. Wide angle lenses will tend to make each item smaller and spread out the picture so that objects appear further from each other, both horizontally and in depth, than they would to the normal eye. The reverse is true when telephoto lenses are used. Different filters and film emulsions, whether black and white or color, vary the color values on prints and transparencies. The angle or elevation from which a picture is taken can affect truthful rendition and magnify or minimize obstructions. It is found that in some situations foreground items on a photographic print look nearer on the left than on the right. Items in the background do not follow this rule.[41]

Comparative brightness may indicate movement. Since brightness has some of the constant characteristics of size and will dominate those "cues" of lesser constancy, when the strength of a pinpoint of light is varied in a darkened room the observer concludes that the point is moving, toward him when it becomes brighter, away when it becomes dimmer.[42] Brightness may also be taken as a cue to distance. Early astronomers, for example, assumed that the brightest stars were certainly closest to the earth. Since there was no experiential information about the actual size of a star, its brightness was taken as an indication of its distance from the observer.

Motion, in terms of *direction and velocity*, has also been found to be governed largely by cues of size and overlay, overlay being the apparent sequence of objects in space as related to the observer, indicated by what commonly appears to be the obstructed perception of one object by another object seemingly nearer to the observer. This has been demonstrated by the famous experiments with the "rotating trapezoid," a two-dimensional representation of what appears to be a window frame in perspective. The perceptual conflicts that arise when the "frame" is rotated while an object moves on a straight line through one of the "panes" create a dissonance in perceptions that most observers resolve by rationalizing the motion. In this case the overlay produced by the object (in these experiments

---

[41] Bartley & DeHardt, *A Further Factor in Determining Nearness as a Function of Lateral Orientation in Pictures,* 50 J. PSYCHOLOGY 53-57 (1960); Bartley & DeHardt, *Phenomenal Distance in Scenes with Independent Manipulation of Major and Minor Items, id.* at 315.
[42] Kilpatrick & Ittelson, *supra* note 39.

a playing card) and the rotating trapezoid conflicted with and dominated the constant size, speed, and direction of the object, leading to the rationalization by the observer that the size, speed, and direction of the object had been varied during the experiment.[43]

But as Ames, who developed this rotating trapezoid, reported, certain characteristics of it will be seen by all observers, and others will vary with the viewer's locus in time and space. For example, the experience of all viewers was so strong in terms of perspective that they were unable to accept the rotation of the trapezoid because that would have placed the side of the "window" that should have been farther away nearer to them. They therefore observed the rotating motion as an oscillation, even when a cube was attached to the trapezoid to indicate its actual motion by creating overlay. Furthermore, when the trapezoid was at rest, if the *observer* moved slightly to the right or left the trapezoid appeared to be in motion.

Observation of velocity is especially difficult, and practically every automobile accident case produces testimonial variations of from five to twenty-five percent as to speed. Extensive experience in driving or watching moving vehicles will increase the observer's likelihood of accuracy. In general, the perception of the rate of tangential motion is easier to gauge than motion toward or away from the viewer.[44] A test among air force personnel found that even among observers who knew in advance that they were to estimate the speed of a moving car the guesses ranged from ten to fifty miles per hour, even though the car was in fact going at only twelve miles per hour.[45] Other tests mentioned in the same report show that a car's color, body style, and noise influence the witness's estimate of speed. Parenthetically, the body size and style of a car may relate to biases in the observer, some people apparently being biased against large cars, others against small ones or convertibles. Weight is a frequent issue in tort and criminal cases. It appears that color influences perception of weight

---

[43] Kilpatrick & Ittelson, *supra* note 39; also Ames, *The Rotating Trapezoid: Description of Phenomena*, in EXPLORATIONS IN TRANSACTIONAL PSYCHOLOGY 222 (Kilpatrick ed. 1961).

[44] Gardner, *supra* note 40.

[45] 3, No. 12 AMERICAN SOCIETY FOR PUBLIC ADMINISTRATION BULL. 4 (1959).

as well as estimates of speed, apparent brightness being a major cue to estimates of weight.[46]

Just as experience gives rise to expectations that are used to fill the gaps in hearing, so experience and expectation fill blanks in perceptions of motion. We expect that "movement will occur in the direction in which previous presentation [or the same or a similar situation] was perceived to move." [47] This finding is particularly applicable to converging traffic and the movements of persons at the scene of an occurrence involved in litigation.

Filling gaps in perception is a betting process. We select what we believe will be harmonious with those elements we have perceived and repress those that will create conflicts for us. The elements that we choose or repress will depend on what bet,[48] or what selection, we make as the likeliest explanation for what we see; and that bet will, of course, be conditioned by past experience in similar situations.

The rotating trapezoid has been used in many ingenious ways to demonstrate our need to reconcile conflicts in what we think we see with what we know from experience. One of the most compelling demonstrates how easy it is to condition the observer's assumptions, or rationalizations, that perceptual conflicts will necessitate. Each observer is handed a steel cylinder to feel and return to the experimenter who is to place it perpendicular to the rotating trapezoid within one of the "panes." This process is then repeated with a rubber cylinder, and the viewer is asked to describe the motion he has observed. More than half of the observers saw a difference in the motion in the two situations, with most reporting some lengthening or cutting through of the "window" by the first cylinder (presumed to be steel) and some bending of the second cylinder (presumed to be rubber) as it and the trapezoid rotated. In fact, the experimenter had inserted a plastic cylinder in both cases, but the suggestion created by the known, experienced characteristics of steel and rubber respectively justi-

---

[46] Payne, Jr., *Apparent Weight as a Function of Color*, 71 AMERICAN J. PSYCHOLOGY 725-30 (1958). See also Payne, Jr., *Apparent Weight as a Function of Hue*, 74 *id.* (1961), at 104.
[47] Krampen & Toch, *The Determination of Perceived Movement Direction*, 50 J. PSYCHOLOGY 271-77 (1960).
[48] See Ittelson, *The Constancies of Visual Perception*, in EXPLORATIONS IN TRANSACTIONAL PSYCHOLOGY 339-51 (Kilpatrick ed. 1961).

fied for the viewer two different reconciliations of the apparent disparity in motion perceived. Kilpatrick describes this necessary reconciliation as the product of the observer's repression of the element that he believes to have created the conflict.[49]

This "betting" process as an element in perception has been described by Ittelson as "the product of the continual recoding of the relatedness of things as defined by action . . . the apprehension of *probable* significance." [50] This is further indicated by Toch's finding that all observers who realized that objects briefly flashed on a slide were bombs believed that they saw the objects depicted as falling. Those who properly identified vertical airplanes, nose up, saw them as soaring upward.[51]

At this point we might also notice a cue that is a variation on overlay-perspective. That we tend to construct the third dimension of a special relationship between two objects on the basis of their two-dimensional relationship is especially apparent in experiments with parallel vertical lines; two lines of different lengths, the bottom of the shorter one lower than the bottom of the longer one, will be perceived as lines of different sizes at the same distance from the

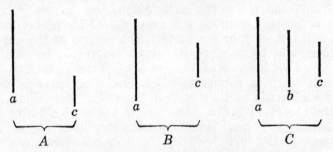

Reproduced from Explorations in Transactional Psychology (1961)
by permission of New York University Press.

viewer. But, if the midpoints of the two are at the same level, then they will appear to be the same size but at a different distance from the observer. In the latter case, the assumption of same size and different distance is reinforced by adding a third parallel line between the two and

[49] Kilpatrick, *Assumptions and Perceptions: Three Experiments,* *id.* at 257, 276-87.

[50] Ittelson, *supra* note 48.

[51] See Krampen & Toch, *supra* note 47.

intermediate in size and space.[52] This process by which we take a chance on the probable significance of perception can be treated also in terms of expectation calling for reinforcement or release of some tension.[53]

Let us consider expectation the readiness for reinforcement of some need. Need is a tension in a human system and at the same time a motive or drive for some conscious or unconscious behavior. What one's expectation or readiness for reinforcement in a particular instance will be relates to: (1) his need to be reinforced; (2) his estimate of the "probability of occurrence of [a possible] . . . outcome"; and (3) his estimate of the ". . . desirability of [the] outcome." [54] What this means in terms of motivation of parties to a proceeding and witnesses will be discussed later.[55] At this point it is only necessary to say that expectation, such readiness for reinforcement, determines the "bet" made to explain what has been seen or heard and offered as testimony. Thus if we have a need, a motive, to identify the man who committed the theft, and the man the police show us is sufficiently similar in appearance to be the probable thief, and we believe it desirable to identify the thief, we tend to have a readiness to be reinforced in our identification by the very fact that the police show us such a man in the lineup. Similarly our belief that we crossed the intersection while the light was green is supported by the expectation that we could not have gone against a red light because our experience tells us that we always stop on red.

The compelling force of experience upon the observer is explained psychologically in terms of the past successes in similar perception. This is an essentially pragmatic process, *i.e.*, if in the past this particular assumption has been validated by action, then it has been tested, it "works," and it should remain as at least a working hypothesis until some strong challenge to it is presented that will dictate the application of a different set of experiences. In this way man adjusts to his environment, clinging to that which is familiar and avoiding the unfamiliar by distorting it to fit into his previous perceptual framework. That is why

---

[52] Kilpatrick, *The Nature of Perception: Some Visual Demonstrations, op. cit. supra* note 48, at 36, 44.

[53] MURPHY, PERSONALITY 89 (1947).

[54] STOGDILL, INDIVIDUAL BEHAVIOR AND GROUP ACHIEVEMENT 63 (1959).

[55] See text, pp. 85-86 *infra*.

the cues that are most often valid will dominate our perception, and those that are most variable will be subordinated.

It must be remembered in considering all of these "cues," or characteristics, though, that none of them is an attribute of the object itself independent of the beholder. All are derived from his total experience as brought to bear on a particular perception.

There is, as we have all experienced, no constancy to an individual's perception. The beholder, the witness, is not the identical person at different times. Some people who see well in daylight are aware that they do not see as clearly as others at dusk. Alcohol, drugs, exhaustion and emotional states such as anxiety affect perception. Age may make a difference. Older persons, it has been found, are poorer judges spacially and have less accurate depth perception than middle aged persons. Perception of verticals may also differ at varying ages. This may mean that in a specific situation conflicting testimony is not caused by dishonesty, angle of view or other opportunity but is the result of chronological age of the various witnesses.[55a] It has been found that menstruation and the premenstruum affect accident-proneness in women, probably because they are "responsible for a lowered judgment and slow reaction time." [55b]

The physiological condition of a witness is a relevant variable in determining the accuracy of his testimony. But, except in patent cases of drunkenness, drug addiction, hysteria, senility or youth, the trial process is not geared to evaluate the effects of physiological conditions on perception or the inconstancy of the capacity to perceive.

2. INTERPRETIVE JUDGMENTS AND SIGNIFICANCE.

We have discussed the inadequacies of perception common to all witnesses, and know that we are not free to interpret our perceptions without reference to our experience. Beyond this are the specific limitations such as color-blindness, nearsightedness or farsightedness, binocular or binaural imbalance, and other physiological conditions that may be unique to certain individuals. Just as percep-

---

[55a] Chown & Heron, *Psychological Aspects of Aging in Man*, ANNUAL REVIEW OF PSYCHOLOGY 435-36 (1965).

[55b] Dalton, *Menstruation and Accidents*, BRITISH MEDICAL J. 1425-26 (1960).

tion is colored by the past, giving rise to the expectation that what has been will be repeated, so interpretation makes use of values that have demonstrated their validity in similar transactions, happenings, or events to give significance to the present. In other words, what we call interpretation is similar to the transactional nature of perception; perhaps it is a phase of it—a more conscious application of the same process by which we read into our perceptions of distance the cue offered by experience with the size of objects in the environment.

An example of interpretive judgment is found in Chapter II where people inferred that the woman in a picture was the mother of the baby because she had called out, "My baby!" She did nothing of the sort, but by assigning this significance to the scene the viewers attained a sense of constancy between what they had seen and what they expected. We do this daily off the witness stand as well as on it. Life would be difficult without such interpretive judgments. However, they make difficult an accurate determination of objective reality.

Interpretive judgments are conditioned not only by the observer's experience as *a* human being but as a *particular* human being. They are not only the product of limitations of sense perception that are common to all of us but also of the unique characteristics of the individual. The significances he assigns to things and happenings are the result of his values and of subjective attitudes that may be derived from his age, race, nationality, sex, profession, religion—all his lifetime experience.

Thus we move from the primarily physiological to the social level, and can observe here the same search for external constancy. Constancy has been defined as "the sum total of the estimates one has, based on past experience, of one's own capacities to deal with particular sets of impingements."[56] What this means is that the individual will generalize in order to establish unity of self and his society. He will see and establish patterns and tools for unifying various kinds of human behavior. "All of these significances that we build up about the self and about objects, people, events, symbols, or ideas fuse and orchestrate to give us our own unique reality world. Everything that has significances for us takes on its significances from our personal

---

[56] Kilpatrick & Cantril, *supra* note 20, at 357-58.

behavior center—in terms of our own purposes and our own actions," and, of course, expectations. "In other words, behavior is seen as ultimately aimed at a state categorized as 'equilibrium.' " [57]

How interpretation is affected by and gives significance to an observer's commitment or loyalty is further illustrated by an experiment of Hastorf and Cantril. They showed students at Dartmouth and Princeton the official film of a particularly rough football game between the two colleges. The men of each college, ascribing different reasons for the claims of the other that the game was "rough and dirty," tended to see the infractions of the rules by their team very differently from the other school's men.[58]

The emphasis on the subjective is not meant to portray an exaggerated atomization of society in which each person is isolated by virtue of his unique nature. There is inevitably communication and the shared experience of a culture and of all the subcultural units that exist in a society. This emphasis is intended to demonstrate the unreliability of any single set of perceptions or interpretations, because they are a product of individual assumptions derived from experience. In the selection process involved we choose for our *attention* happenings related to our *intention*.[59]

Filling gaps in perception is a betting process. We select what we believe will be harmonious with those elements we have perceived and repress those that will create dissonance for us. *The elements that we choose or repress will depend on what bet,*[60] *or what selection, we make as the likeliest explanation for what we see; and that bet will, of course, be conditioned by past experience in similar situations.*[61]

---

[57] Kilpatrick & Cantril, *id.* at 363; Toch & Hastorf, *Homeostasis in Psychology, A Review and Critique* 18, 1 PSYCHIATRY: JOURNAL FOR THE STUDY OF INTERPERSONAL PROCESSES 89, 90 (1955).

[58] Hastorf & Cantril, *They Saw a Game: A Case Study,* 49, No. 1 J. ABNORMAL AND SOCIAL PSYCHOLOGY 129-34 (1954).

[59] CANTRIL, THE POLITICS OF DESPAIR 15-18 (1958).

[60] See Ittelson, *The Constancies of Visual Perception, op. cit. supra* note 48.

[61] The rotating trapezoid has been used in many ingenious ways to demonstrate our need to reconcile conflicts in what we think we see with what we know from experience. See text page 18. Kilpatrick, *Assumptions and Perceptions: Three Experiments,* in EXPLORATIONS IN TRANSACTIONAL PSYCHOLOGY, *op. cit. supra* note 48, at 257, 276-87.

Ideally, we should know what constitutes reality to each witness in order to evaluate his evidence. We should know the patterns of his selectivity, how his process of perception selects interpretations of objects and happenings and gives significances to them, and how in turn he interprets his perceptions to form a pattern that will give *him* a needed constancy in his relation to the external world. This is impossible in the adversarial conflict of a courtroom.

B. RECOLLECTION

Considerable transformation of a happening and its initial perception occurs in recollection. (See Chapter II.) To demonstrate the fallibility of memory is one of the chief aims of the cross-examiner. Witnesses are historians and autobiographers; on the witness stand they are reconstructing past events. Many of them to the best of their ability attempt to do it honestly, but it is not strange to find the grossest imperfection even in the memory of an honest man. Not only may his hearing and his eyesight be defective, but all his recollections often are the product of an association of ideas, commingled and confused with rationalization, and "all his memory may be tinctured by a bias, sometimes subconscious, or colored by suggestion." [62] Not only do people vary in their native or trained capacities to recall what has occurred or what they have learned, but recollection is also affected by the circumstances in which the events have occurred, the learning taken place, or the story retold.

Observers commonly see more than they can report. It has been found that "at the time of exposure, and for a few tenths of a second thereafter, observers have two to three times as much information available as they can later report. The availability of this information declines rapidly. . . ." [63] The location of stimuli in the field of vision may affect the degree of an observer's recall as may the sequence with which certain items are reported, for memory is somewhat better with respect to the first items reported than those later reported. It would seem probable, however, that some of the "forgotten" material is suppressed,

---

[62] STRYKER, THE ART OF ADVOCACY 94 (1954).

[63] Sperling, *The Information Available in Brief Visual Presentations*, 74, No. 11 PSYCHOLOGICAL MONOGRAPHS: GENERAL AND APPLIED 1, 26 (1960).

repressed, or subliminal and may be brought back to consciousness by new stimuli, such as direct or cross-examination or the testimony of other witnesses.[64] By the time a witness testifies, the true order or recall has been lost.

Memory, too, is selective. Interrupted tasks may be remembered more frequently than those completed.[65] Individual personality, as one would expect, determines the nature of the selections made. People who are able to be decisive in making decisions "tend to recall more failures than successes." [66] The indecisive recall more successes than failures. For the latter, this serves the function of ego defense when they have been unable to act decisively.[67]

It has also been found that "an individual notes and remembers material which supports his social attitudes better than material which conflicts with these attitudes." The test here involved two statements, one very anti-Soviet, the other pro-Soviet. Two groups of students, one pro-Communist and one anti-Communist (in the early 1940's) read the two statements; the pro-Soviet selection was learned better and forgotten more slowly by the pro-Communist group; and the disparity was the reverse, and even greater, between the pro- and anti-Communists' retention of the anti-Soviet statement.[68] This again is a process of selection and "denial."

The time interval between the crime, the accident or other cause of action and the trial is usually several months, if not years. During that interval the witness's impression of the incident is subject to numerous stresses. Foremost is what we call the "curve of forgetting," a leveling-out

---

[64] *Id.* at 27. See also Schiff, *The Effects of Subliminal Stimuli on Guessing Accuracy*, 74 AMERICAN J. PSYCHOLOGY 54-60 (1961).

[65] Zeigarnik, *Das Behalten erledigter Handlugen*, 9 PSYCHOLOGISCHE FORSCHUNG 1-85 (1927), cited by Horowitz, *The Recall of Interrupted Group Tasks: An Experimental Study of Individual Motivation in Relation to Group Goals*, in CARTWRIGHT & ZANDER, GROUP DYNAMICS: RESEARCH AND THEORY 370-94 (2d ed. 1960).

[66] Horowitz, *Psychological Need as a Function of Social Environments*, in THE STATE OF THE SOCIAL SCIENCES 162-79 (White ed. 1956).

[67] See *id.* at 176-80.

[68] Levine & Murphy, *The Learning and Forgetting of Controversial Material*, in READINGS IN SOCIAL PSYCHOLOGY 94-101 (Maccoby, Newcomb & Hartley 3d ed. 1958). See also Bartlett, *Social Factors in Recall*, in *id.* at 47, 53.

process in which most of what happens is forgotten within a matter of hours or days.[69] (See Chapter II.)

The intensity of the impression is also governed by its emotional impact. For example, the ordinary occurrence is less memorable than the unusual; it is essentially neutral because it makes no new demand upon the perceptual adjustments an observer makes to incorporate the occurrence in his framework of experience.[70]

We know too little about the relation of stress to recollection to form a working principle. However, it seems that under social stress those percepts which are most familiar are remembered best. "Whenever strong, preferred, persistent social tendencies are subjected to any form of social control . . . social remembering is very apt to take on a constructive and inventive character, either wittingly or unwittingly. Its manner then tends to become assertive, rather dogmatic and confident, and recall will probably be accompanied by excitement and emotion." [71]

It is not only the stress arising out of the incident reported that affects testimony. Most witnesses, of course, are under tension caused by internal and external pressures of the courtroom situation. Lewis Carroll captured the feeling of a witness taking the stand by having the King of Hearts say to the witness: "Give your evidence, and don't be nervous, or I'll have you executed on the spot." [72] This is particularly understandable on cross-examination, which may well be described as a duel between a cross-examiner and a witness.

The kind of detail that a witness is asked to report generally falls into the category of "incidental memory." Hugo Münsterberg asked a class of 100 students to observe one hand while spinning a color wheel with the other and

---

[69] See Hutchins & Slesinger, *op. cit. supra* note 9. Diminution of accuracy through rumor is like that of the curve of forgetting, with the number of details eliminated at once being greatest. A sharpening process occurs, in which unusual words or episodes are retained and may be elaborated upon; there is also a leveling, or condensing, taking place, and assimilation by the hearer of that which he hears of his own experience. The last is the major source of distortion. Leveling, sharpening, and assimilation occur simultaneously, and result in the "falsification . . . so characteristic of rumor." Allport & Postman, *The Basic Psychology of Rumor*, in READINGS IN SOCIAL PSYCHOLOGY 54, 65 (Maccoby, Newcomb & Hartley 3d ed. 1958).

[70] See Bartlett, *op. cit. supra* note 68, at 53.

[71] *Ibid.*

[72] CARROLL, *op. cit. supra* note 29.

18 students reported seeing only the spinning color wheel. Münsterberg also staged in his classroom the classic incident in which a prearranged but unannounced battle took place, culminating in the firing of a shot. The variations in the accounts of the incident written immediately afterward are great, but not random. Those most upset by the episode were least accurate in reporting it, those totally unaffected were somewhat more accurate, and those who were moderately involved emotionally were most accurate in reporting. These were untrained and unprepared observers, presumably with no stake in either side of the sham conflict.[73] Even experienced observers whose attention has already been drawn to a shock-producing episode will differ in their observations. For example, Hutchins and Slesinger excerpt an editorial from *The New York World* that described the great disparities in eight newspaper reports of a simple situation in which Kerensky, on the speaker's platform, was slapped. The eight published reports all differed as to the sequence of events, Kerensky's reaction, and other integral aspects of a simple, brief, and unique episode.[74]

We can easily speculate on how much greater the variations would have been if the accounts had been written a year later, or after discussing the incident with others who had been present, or at the request of one of the parties to the conflict. Yet such accounts are usually the basis for determining liability — after an automobile accident for example — and criminal guilt.

We realize that a person's recall of a conversation reflects his interpretation of what took place, the selective process discussed above.[75] This interpretation-selection will be in terms of the person's expectations, but there is frequently difficulty in determining what his expectations are. What is his estimate of the probabilities of what was said? What is his estimate of the desirability of an outcome? It is such questions that determine the form taken by selective

---

[73] This experiment is reported in Hutchins & Slesinger, *Some Observations on the Law of Evidence*, 28 COLUM. L. REV. 432, 437 (1928). And see MÜNSTERBERG, ON THE WITNESS STAND: ESSAYS IN PSYCHOLOGY AND CRIME 15-36, 50 (1923) and PSYCHOLOGY: GENERAL AND APPLIED 396, ch. 30 (1915).

[74] Hutchins & Slesinger, *op. cit. supra* note 73, at 438.

[75] See text accompanying notes 21-23 *supra*. Also, Touster, *Law and Psychology, How the Twain Might Meet*, 5 AMERICAN BEHAVIORAL SCIENTIST 3 (1962).

memory. "It is not always safe to rely upon a person's verbal report of his expectations because custom and convention make it difficult or embarrassing to express certain kinds of hopes and ambitions, particularly those which might conflict with the interests of other persons. . . ." [76]

A rule permitting *refreshment of recollection* is a further legal recognition of the imperfections of memory. But allowance of such refreshment assumes that the recollection thus refreshed will be essentially accurate, that it is latent in the witness's mind and will be brought to the fore, intact, by his seeing or hearing an echo of the initial occurrence. The witness may be shown something he had written soon after the incident. Then he may "recall" either his original observation or, at least, having written it down at that time. Although this may meet the problem of the fallibility of memory, it leaves open the basic question whether the observation was accurate in the first instance.

The "refreshment of recollection" that the law permits deals with that "refreshment" conducted in the courtroom, before the judge and jury. But it cannot be doubted that the more common form of refreshment takes place before the trial, when the attorney prepares the case and interviews the witnesses. As the *Columbia Report* observed, "The distinction between coaching witnesses and preparing a case for trial is unfortunately too fine to be universally observed. Even deliberate perjury is resorted to; witnesses sometimes testify to the details of an accident they have never seen, or deliberately lie about the things they have seen." [77] The authors of that report, leading members of the bar, asserted that witnesses to motor vehicle accidents were especially susceptible to such pressures.

The impact of *suggestion* on recollection cannot be exaggerated. It is known to the law and social science in numerous forms. "Refreshment" can be suggestion; it can also increase the distortion of memory. An instance noted by Hutchins and Slesinger[78] was an experiment in which all those present at an event were asked soon after to write a

---

[76] See STOGDILL, *op. cit. supra* note 54, at 63-64.

[77] COMM. TO STUDY COMPENSATION FOR AUTOMOBILE ACCIDENTS; REPORT TO THE COLUMBIA UNIVERSITY COUNCIL FOR RESEARCH IN THE SOCIAL SCIENCES 38 (1932).

[78] Hutchins & Slesinger, *Some Observations on the Law of Evidence—Memory*, 41 HARV. L. REV. 860, 869 (1928).

report of it. Some of them had also been allowed to read
an inaccurate newspaper account of it. Those who read
the newspaper account described the event as it was reported; those who did not read the story presented far
more accurate accounts based on their own unrefreshed
recollections.

Scientific reports have indicated that the witness's spontaneous narrative is more accurate (as well as more interesting and more impressive to a jury) than his testimony
in response to step-by-step interrogation, although the latter may be more complete. The danger here is that the
witness may acquiesce in a false suggestion. It is for this
reason that in general "leading" questions may not be asked
of one's own witness; but the definition of leading is far
from precise.[79]

Though counsel may not lead his own witness and thus,
in effect, testify through him, opposing counsel is free to
suggest testimony under cross-examination by means of
leading questions. Leading questions are permitted on
cross-examination on the theory that broad scope must be
given in order to test memory, veracity, and accuracy. It
was undoubtedly an improvement to permit the impeach-
ment of witnesses and no longer to accept as true their
statements because they were under oath.[80] We have made
progress by eliminating the mystical quality of early evidentiary proof, such as the oath, ordeal, and battle. Still,
one might well subject to empirical research the question
of the degree to which answers suggested by the cross-
examiner distort the witness's report of what he observed
and recalled.

We still require far more data than is available to understand the effects of *suggestion*.[81] However, we do have
certain findings about interaction between and among people, which are relevant here. We know that some people
are more susceptible to suggestion than others. For example, a person who is oriented to personalities—one who

[79] McCormick, Laws of Evidence (1954).
[80] See 2 Pollock & Maitland, The History of English Law
600 (2d ed. 1898).
[81] *But see* Asch, *The Effects of Group Pressures Upon the Modification and Distortion of Judgments*, in Cartwright & Zander, *op.
cit. supra* note 65, at 189; Siegel & Siegel, *Reference Groups, Membership Groups, and Attitude Change*, in Cartwright & Zander,
op. cit. supra note 65, at 232; and Sherif, The Psychology of Social
Norms 96-108 (1936).

tends to get cues for his beliefs and actions from people with authority or status or others from whom he needs psychological support—is more likely to be susceptible to the cues given by others than "content-oriented" personalities, those who get their cues from the phenomena of the problems which they face.[82] Consequently, a witness oriented to personalities will look to the judge for cues and when he gets none will look to the attorney who is examining or cross-examining him, to another witness, or even to a newspaper account of the case. The content-oriented witness will tend to seek his cues from events and objects, however imperfect his perceptions, rather than from persons; although it is improbable any normal person would be completely free from the effects of interaction with others.

From this we see that the "reality" brought to the case is a function not only of the perception of the witness but also of his individual personality and of situation, including the situation of the event testified to, the situation of the preparation of the case for trial, and the situation of the courtroom.

It is assumed that cross-examination will bring out truth and unveil false or inaccurate testimony. While it is true that a witness can be challenged on the accuracy of his observation, the point here made is not that the observation of the individual witness may be at fault but that on the whole the observation of all witnesses is faulty in some degree or in some situations. We bring to our observation of events preconceptions based upon experience. Our experience gives rise in us to expectations which color what we observe. And cognitive knowledge of the facts does not necessarily act to correct faulty observation.

For example, the author had read about the perceptual experiments used in the *Ames* demonstrations before he saw them (including the trapezoid mentioned on page 18, the distorted room, the lights of varying brightness, etc.).[83] Nevertheless, as had been the case with many other observers of the exhibition, his perceptions were as inaccurate as those of persons who had no knowledge of the exhibits

---

[82] See McDavid, Jr., *Personality and Situational Determinants of Conformity*, 58 J. ABNORMAL AND SOCIAL PSYCHOLOGY 241, 246 (1959).

[83] These demonstrations devised by the late Adelbert Ames, Jr. and set up by Professor Hadley Cantril at Princeton in connection with his pioneer work in transactional psychology, and removed to Brooklyn College, include the trapezoid above mentioned, the distorted room, the lights of varying brightness, etc.

before seeing them. Expectations on the cognitive level were not sufficient to overcome expectations on the observational level. In the distorted room the face in the small window appeared larger than the face in the large window.

Reproduced from Explorations in Transactional Psychology, New York University Press (1961), by permission of the author, M. Lawrence, Studies in Human Behavior (1949), and the Publisher, Princeton University Press.

The brighter light looked closer than the dimmer light although in fact they were at the same distance. This does not mean that if faced with the need to act the author would not have resolved the incongruity existing between his observation and his cognition by choosing the latter as the determining factor in taking action. That assumes that he would have both time for recognition and for resolution of the incongruity. But if he had to act instantaneously, as the driver of a car or a pedestrian generally must, it would be the inaccurate observation which would control his behavior.

Psychological findings indicate that there is no evidence that a person will behave in the same way in all situations. Each situation, including interaction with other people, affects behavior; and different variables in each situation may cause different behavior by the same person. Thus, a man who will tell the truth and be shocked at the assertion that he could do anything but tell the truth under oath might well commit perjury in another circumstance. This should throw doubt upon the rule that "character for truth is always and everywhere admissible." Wigmore explains the relevance of the rule on the ground that the probability of telling the truth can be evaluated by the witness's "quality or tendency as to truth-telling in general, *i.e.*, his *veracity*, or, as more commonly and more loosely put, his *character for truth*." [84] This would assume that "character" is consistent and independent of the pressures of the situation and the witness's interaction with others involved.

It is often assumed, too, that people always know when they are not telling the truth. False testimony can sometimes be based on false memories and perceptions which are frequently symptomatic of mental illness. For example, "The need to sacrifice another human being at the altar of one's guilt-laden conscience is one of the difficult sources of memory distortion which enter into all cases in which someone who has confessed guilt of past crimes turns and accuses others, whether of private offenses, criminal acts or acts of treason and subversion." [85]

False testimony may be intentional and conscious; on the other hand it may involve *psychological denial* by the witness that he is testifying falsely, that is, he may be blocking out the truth and not recognize he is doing so. Freud explained this process by his finding that "the ego often finds itself in the position of warding off some claim from the *external world* which it feels as painful, and that this is affected by *denying* the perceptions that bring to knowledge such a demand on the part of reality." [86] Doctor Lewin in discussing Freud's concept adds, "Denial disclaims the external world, then, as repression disclaims the instincts." [87]

Festinger suggests that where there is "a cluster of cognitive elements corresponding to some very important action a person has taken, an action to which he has committed himself in such a way that changing the action is

[84] 3 WIGMORE, EVIDENCE § 922, at 447 (3d ed. 1940).
[85] Kubie, *Implications for Legal Procedure of the Fallibility of Human Memory*, 108 U. PA. L. REV. 59-75, at 70 (1959).
[86] FREUD, AN OUTLINE OF PSYCHOANALYSIS 118 (1949).
[87] LEWIN, THE PSYCHOANALYSIS OF ELATION 52-53 (1950).

almost impossible," something may occur that impinges
on this person's cognition, creating a strong dissonance
with the cognition. If he cannot successfully reduce such
a conflict-dissonance by acquiring new evidence or arguments in support of the original cognition, he will probably
attempt to deny the validity of the event which caused the
dissonance.[88]

We see this when a witness who has told his story on
direct examination is confronted with conflicting statements made by himself or other witnesses. In his desire
not to look foolish the witness may change his testimony
that now seems to him neither logical nor sensible. On the
other hand, he may feel he has "committed himself in such
a way that changing the action" is impossible. The more
often he has had to repeat his testimony the more he will
tend to believe it and find it impossible to change what he
said. The contradictory statements with which he is confronted, which create a conflict with what he has testified,
may cause him to deny the existence of the dissonant, the
contradictory statements. *This denial* is not a simple ver-
balized denial—not just saying "No"—but an ego defense
causing him to block out recognition that the contradictory
statements are realities. Such behavior *should* properly
discredit a witness—not as a perjurer, but because he is
denying reality; however, presumably to the triers of fact,
he will appear to be a perjurer, not a mere incredible
witness.

The fusing and multiplying of experiences also occur
and reduce the accuracy of recall.

> "In one emotional state multiple experiences can
> be fused and then be represented in memory as though
> they had been one event. This happens constantly in
> childhood, as when a child may recall as a single start-
> ling event something that may have happened a hun-
> dred times. This is one form of what is called tech-
> nically a 'screen memory.' Every adult does this too.
> On the other hand, that same child or adult may recall
> one single event as though it had happened many
> times. This is another potential source of guileless
> discrepancies in juridical testimony." [89]

Few witnesses testify without advance knowledge of
what details would be most helpful to the party for whom

[88] FESTINGER, A THEORY OF COGNITIVE DISSONANCE 235-43 (1957).
[89] Kubie, *op. cit. supra* note 85, at 68.

they are testifying. The witness's recollection is affected
by the fact that he has been asked to testify by a particular
participant, and therefore the witness's interest becomes
entwined with that of the party for whom he appears
(see Chapter II). These are "adversary" proceedings, and
if *his* side wins the witness shares in a form of social re-
ward that reinforces his "self-constancy." Unless he is
merely answering a subpoena duces tecum, he can rarely
avoid identifying with one side or the other, and the result
will be either the endorsement of his commitment resulting
from success of *his* party or frustration through failure of
his side.[90]

With regard to criminal cases, reference has already
been made to the suggestive effects of the police lineup in
identification of suspects. In many instances the victim is
especially susceptible to suggestions by the police or the
district attorney because in his hostile state toward an
offender he is eager to find a likely object for his hostility.
A witness for the prosecution in a criminal case usually
wants to be helpful. Sometimes there is a threat, or at
least he feels a threat, if he does not cooperate with the
prosecutor. Accomplices and co-conspirators are particularly susceptible to pressures by the prosecution. They have
something to gain, they hope, by being cooperative.

The prosecutor may find conflicting pieces of evidence
on specific detail, and he must put together a consistent
story. The same is true of the attorney for the defense and
attorneys in civil cases. If the attorney can bring the witnesses together, each witness tends to be influenced substantially by what the others have said in his presence, or
if they are not present, by what the attorney represents
that the other witnesses have said. By making the parts
fit together there is a reduction of contradictory elements
and thus of tension.[91]

Moreover, no witness wants to look foolish. He wants,
wherever possible, not to be in conflict with other witnesses
on his side. If others are saying something slightly different from what he has said, his confidence in his own

---

[90] Kilpatrick & Cantril, *The Constancies in Social Perception*, in
EXPLORATIONS IN TRANSACTIONAL PSYCHOLOGY 354 (Kilpatrick ed.
1961).

[91] Festinger & Aronson, *The Arousal and Reduction of Dissonance
in Social Contexts*, in CARTWRIGHT & ZANDER, *op. cit. supra* note 65,
at 214.

perceptions tends to be weakened and his confidence that
the views of others may be the correct ones increases. He is
then likely to deny the evidence of his own senses and alter
his beliefs to concur with those of others.[92] This same
process—the weakening of confidence in one's own belief—
also occurs, as we shall see, in the jury room.

When a witness identifies with one side of a case it is
similar to becoming a member of a group. In effect his
"group" is composed of a party and other witnesses on the
side of the case for which he is testifying. It has been found
that there is a tendency to assume beliefs of the members
of the group which one joins. So, too, the witness gains
reinforcement from supporting the beliefs of his side.[93]

William A. White said: "An unprejudiced individual
does not exist." This, of course, was the theory of Khru-
shchev in proposing a troika in place of the Secretary General of the United Nations to replace Dag Hammarskjöld.
Nevertheless, changing one's role may change one's prejudices [94] (or cause one to be more aware of and more on
guard against them). Use of scientific method reduces
prejudice to a minimum, because its essence is that all
experiments must be subject to replication by others. So
that unless all the experimenters shared in the same prejudice the results would not check out.

Just as observation may be influenced by what the observer feels would be to his advantage, so a witness who
knows that it would be advantageous if he were to re-
member that the light was red, or that the fire engine was
sounding its siren, or the suspect had declared his intention
to avenge himself on the victim, may ultimately believe that
this was what he saw or heard. Thus a woman sitting with
her rear over the window ledge cleaning her third-story
window while elevated trains were passing testified she
heard the defendant on the street threaten to kill the victim
just before the shot was fired. She volunteered her testimony
to the district attorney and was a neighborhood heroine.
She came to this observation when she read that the de-

---

[92] Asch, *Effects of Group Pressures Upon the Modification and
Distortion of Judgments*, in CARTWRIGHT & ZANDER, *op. cit. supra*
note 65, at 189.

[93] Siegel & Siegel, *Reference Groups, Membership Groups, and
Attitude Change*, in CARTWRIGHT & ZANDER, *op. cit. supra* note 65,
at 232.

[94] Lark, *How Foremen Get That Way*, DUNN'S REVIEW & MODERN
INDUSTRY, Jan. 1955; FESTINGER, *op. cit. supra* note 88, at 274.

fendant and the defendant's former paramour had been talking together on the corner just before the defendant fired the shots. What would have been more natural, then, than that she had threatened to kill him? (P.S. The lady was acquitted.) Interestingly, in the same case a woman detective testified falsely to a conversation several days before the killing in which she claimed the defendant threatened to commit murder and when asked to produce her police report and the police blotter presented a false report which she had typed during the course of her testimony. If either story had been believed the lady might have burned.[95] If a witness's actual recollection is vague or nonexistent then any dissonance or contradiction can be removed or any void filled by slight but welcome advantage to himself, especially some psychological ego advantage.[96]

C. ARTICULATION

The final stage at which the witness's account may be distorted is in its *articulation*. After he has seen, interpreted, and recalled the incident, he must convert his mental image into words that will communicate this image to his hearers. This translation of images into words leads to two kinds of distortion: the use of words creates a compulsion to fill in the gaps in a narrative, and gives no indication to the hearer of how clear to the witness is the image that he is reporting. Words fail to describe accurately the perception they report, or whether it is in effect an inference and not a percept. For instance, if the witness says, "It was raining and I wore my rubbers," we cannot know whether he recalls one of those facts and infers the other, recalls both, or has deduced both from a third recollection, *e.g.*, that he saw people carrying umbrellas.[97]

Language itself, Kilpatrick and Cantril believe, serves as a rigidifying process, creating "slippage between the abstraction as it *functions* in behavior and abstraction as it is *named*. There is a basic tendency to treat whatever is perceived as both concrete and absolute, despite its abstract and nonabsolute nature. To do otherwise is to in-

---

[95] See LEVY, MY DOUBLE LIFE 159-62 (1958).

[96] Cohen, *Attitudinal Consequences of Induced Discrepancies Between Cognition and Behavior*, 24 PUBLIC OPINION Q. 297 (1960).

[97] Hutchins & Slesinger, *op. cit. supra* note 78, at 860, 867.

hibit the rapid and effective action necessary to the process
of living." [98] Words are, of course, symbolic of objective
realities and ideals. They are a shorthand, an essential
but incomplete method of communicating individual experience. As symbols, they connote different experiences to
different persons. It is not possible to reproduce in words
the overtones and prismatic colors, and particularly the
feeling, of the situation described. Court and jury get at
best a reproduction of an abstract.

One is reminded of the various uses of language by
Irwin Edman: "Language is a scandalously ambiguous
instrument. It is a way of describing objective and veri-
fiable things, in the context of practical control, or it is a
lyric cry, an automatic soliloquy. It is sometimes statistics
and sometimes song." [99] And, we might add, sometimes a
screen to true thought and feeling.

Accent and pronunciation may also result in misperceptions. Recently at a meeting a speaker was referring to a
"ten-year plan," but to the author it sounded like "tenure
plan," and it was only after several repetitions that the
author fitted this phrase into context (the expectation of
appropriateness) and understood it as it was intended, not
as it was pronounced.

Other rules of evidence which deserve consideration
relate to declarations against interest, self-serving declarations, and testifying to conclusions. In a psychological sense
a *declaration against interest* (which is admissible in evidence) is just as much a self-serving declaration as any
other such declaration (which the law excludes from evidence), for it is motivated by, and is an expression of, a
need. Because the law searches for guilt or liability rather
than reality or truth as a basis for judgment, it welcomes
confessional evidence and rejects as unreliable attempts at
justification through explanations that are self-defensive.
Neither declarations against interest nor self-serving declarations may be in themselves true, but either may reveal
truth. The circumstances in which they are made and the
turn of their phrasing may illuminate more than their intended meaning. Good cross-examiners have long been
aware of this and since the teachings of Freud have become
common knowledge people have been increasingly alert to

[98] Kilpatrick & Cantril, *op. cit. supra* note 90, at 361.
[99] EDMAN, FOUR WAYS OF PHILOSOPHY 208-09 (1937).

such cues to meaning in daily life. But the rules of the game of litigation are founded on the belief that self-serving declarations will be taken literally and must be excluded.

Similarly, a witness is not trusted to *volunteer* the reasons he comes to a *conclusion, i.e.,* his inferences. (See Chapter II, pp. 50-51.) Instead he is directed to testify to what he saw or heard and he thus frequently testifies to his conclusion as being his observation. Of course, as we have noted, much of observation is a conclusion, a filling in of gaps in perception by experience and expectation. Surely a more accurate evaluation of perception would be possible if the process of filling in gaps and arriving at conclusions were laid on the table. Again, to the psychiatrist and psychologist this process would be just as revealing of reality as any statement of perception and helpful in evaluating the accuracy of a perception.

This detailed account of what we know about how the individual perceives and acts in relation to the world around him indicates some basic flaws in the presumptions which the rules of evidence apply to accounts by witnesses. The disparity between man as a legal concept and as a knowledgeable organism from a scientific view is so great that it serves to make our law seem inappropriate and therefore unworthy of the respect in which we desire it held. Scholars in the area of evidence have been aware of some of the disparities between legal hypotheses and scientific data. McCormick notes, for instance, that the distinction in admissibility between fact and opinion is "clumsy because its basic assumption is an illusion. . . . There is no conceivable statement that is not in some measure the product of inference and reflection as well as observation and memory." [100] He praises courts' increasing flexibility on this matter, although the distinction drawn in this country between inference and memory is more rigid than in England, where it originated.

Courts also have been commended for acknowledging to some extent the scientific findings about recollection and refreshment. The former rule had been that if a witness's prior statement were introduced as conflicting with his testimony on the stand it could be considered only in terms of impeaching the witness's credibility. But courts have been increasingly permissive about the use of the prior statement substantively, since it should in fact have more merit

---

[100] McCormick, *op. cit. supra* note 79.

than the testimony on the stand because it would have been
made earlier.[101]

But this progress in a few limited areas makes more
acute the need for a complete reconsideration of the rules
of evidence to conform them overall instead of piecemeal
to what we know of the human condition. Only in that way
can the law maintain its mediating role in our society. In
fact, this liberalization of certain rules still remains within
the framework of litigation as an adversary proceeding,
rather than as a search for truth.

---

[101] See Hand, J., in DiCarlo v. United States, 6 F.2d 364 (1925)
and in United States v. Block et al., 88 F.2d 618 (1937); also Swan, in
United States v. Corsi, 65 F.2d 564 (1933); and 3 WIGMORE, EVI-
DENCE § 1018(b), at 687 (3d ed. 1940).

CHAPTER II

SOME VAGARIES OF RECALL*

Generally, in the trial of a case there is testimony which concerns a specific happening, that is, certain events which occurred between or among specific individuals at a particular time and place. In tort and criminal cases, witnesses are usually unprepared to see and hear what happens. The situation may be new to them. It usually is. Thus what they perceive and recall and what they may select to perceive and recall among the numerous items in any situation are functions not only of the situation but also of physiological and psychological fields determined by their individual experiences and physical condition.[102] The application to law of some of the empirical evidence already discovered has been reported in Chapter I.

There is a rich if incomplete literature on perception and recall. With few exceptions, however, the experiments reported have involved college students in more or less abstract situations. What has been said of Small Group research is also applicable to research of perception and recall.

"For one, much work is based on very restricted samples, namely, college students. In addition, some research is fairly basic in nature with little interest or attempt by scientists to apply their findings or to initiate studies to solve 'real world' problems."[103]

This research has rarely involved the kind of situation applicable to litigation. Nowhere are perception and recall more intimately related to truth than in the trial of a case.

If law is to be a successful instrument of state policy it is important that its efficacy be demonstrated. It is im-

---

* This chapter is largely based on research done jointly by the author and Helge Mansson, Ph. D. in Social Psychology, with the assistance of John VanEsen.

[102] Kilpatrick & Cantril, *The Constancies in Social Perception*, *op. cit. supra* note 90.

[103] Altman (Naval Medical Research Institute), *Mainstream of Research on Small Groups*, 23, No. 4 PUB. ADMIN. REV. (1963).

portant, too, that there is some approximation of law, as
it is applied by the courts, to legal theory (its premises)
and to moral justifications. The findings of the social psychologists, as noted in the previous chapter, have indicated
serious discrepancies. But since the pioneer work of Münsterberg[104] little has been done to attach the applicability
of those findings to a situation at least approximating such
as may arise in a court. One such situation, experimentally
oriented, dealing with recall, is the subject of their research.

Research by the author and his associates[105] attempted
to study on a quantitative basis some of the factors involved
in the process of recall by witnesses. No attempt was made
to exhaust all possible factors influencing a person's selective
recall. This chapter presents some of the results of their
experiment in which they tried to examine how individuals
of different educational and economic backgrounds perceive
or recall a situation which might occur in the life of any
of us and be the subject at issue in a trial as well as their
misperceptions and inferences. We also attempted to demonstrate the effects of time delays in reporting on what had
been perceived upon selective recall. Other variables will
be discussed later.

A moving picture with sound, lasting 42 seconds, was
shown to 167 law school students in the first month of their
legal training, to 102 police trainees in the first month of
their training in the Police Academy and to 22 people who
attended a settlement house and who lived in low income
housing, and most of whom were on relief, a total of 291
subjects.

Socio-Educational Status of Population Groups

The law students had all completed college and, with
few exceptions, were all of a higher economic level than
the police trainees, very few of whom had had any college
education, but who had all completed high school. The police
trainees, in turn, were of a higher economic level than the
settlement house people, only a few of whom had finished
high school, and about half of whom had not reached high
school.

---

104 MÜNSTERBERG, *op. cit. supra* note 73.
105 See footnote at beginning of ch. II.

Summary of Picture

The picture which we showed had background music through most of the sequence. It opened with a boy lowering a mosquito net on a baby carriage. The boy was in his late teens or early twenties, of average build, wore a dark jacket, lighter baggy slacks, and a white shirt open at the neck. There were white buttons on the jacket and around his neck there were two strings or chains with a flute or whistle on one and a looking glass on the other. He had sideburns, curly hair. The baby was crying. At the beginning, the boy was smiling at the baby carriage. He appeared uncertain or nervous. He faced the baby carriage and touched the handle and started rocking it, then he removed his hands from the handle. The baby cried louder. The boy rocked the baby carriage back and forth, shifting his weight from foot to foot. The rocking became more violent and he pulled the carriage backward off the grass on which it had been to the driveway. A woman called out or shouted, "Mrs. Gerard, Mrs. Gerard, quick! Someone's running away with your baby." The boy turned toward the fence of the yard and then toward the house. A woman came running from the house toward the boy and the carriage. The woman was young. She wore a white smock and a darker skirt. She shouted, "You bad boy! You bad boy!", and waved her left arm as she ran. The boy hesitated, looked startled, ran through the gate and crouched in a corner by a white picket fence near a bush growing through the fence. A mailbox was above his head. At this point the picture stopped.

At the opening the carriage was on the grass in front of the house. The carriage hood was up. It was a four-wheel carriage of a dark color with a patterned design; the mosquito netting covered the hood and open part of the carriage. There was a hem on the mosquito netting. There was a light colored cover in the carriage.

The yard itself had a white picket fence at the left and in front there was a gate and driveway which led to the house. There were three pieces of wicker furniture with cushions in the center of the lawn, two chairs and a settee. There was a tree in the yard and another white picket fence on the side with a shrub or rose bush. It was a time of the year when leaves were on the trees and shrubs.

The subjects of the experiment were asked to consider that they were walking around a corner and what they saw and heard was what they saw and heard in the picture. They were then asked to record what they had perceived. All but a small portion of the law school and police subjects were told that the principal character had been indicted for attempted kidnapping. Half of the subjects were given a bias by being told that he had previously been convicted for molesting children.

Several additional variables were in the pattern of the experiment. The control groups in each of the three populations were asked to write what they had seen and heard. Among the law students, there were also two groups who did the same, one, however, was told that they would be witnesses for the defendant, and another that they would be witnesses for the prosecution. In both the law and the police populations, a group was asked to leave the room and in another room, before the questionnaire was administered to them, they were given a brief talk by a status figure (see pp. 60-63) to see what influence he would have on their recall. Another group of law students and police trainees was taken to rooms where, instead of writing, they spoke into a tape recorder. There was also a group of law students and police trainees who were excused and asked to return a week later, when they were asked to write what they recalled of the picture. All those participating, whether reporting in writing, or orally, were asked a week later again to record what they had seen and heard. It was not possible to have more than a control group for the settlement house people because there was not a sufficient number who consistently attended the sessions.

At the end of the final session, one week after the picture was shown, each subject was given a post-questionnaire to fill out which asked specific questions concerning the film and which will be referred to later.

There were 115 possible items in the picture to be recalled.

We found that in each condition the higher the educational level, the more verbal were the subjects. This was obtained by a word count of the answers to the questionnaires which they filled out, in writing or orally, immediately after seeing the film. The Mean Word Count for

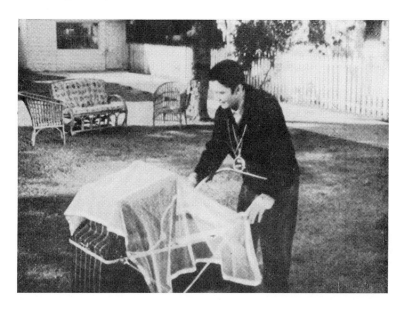

Reproduced with permission of the National Broadcasting Company.

Reproduced with permission of the National Broadcasting Company.

Reproduced with permission of the National Broadcasting Company.

each control group was: Law school 183, police trainees 163, settlement house 77.[106]

It was found that the mean number of items of correct recall and inferences reported are directly related to the amount of education of the subjects. Oral or written, the higher the educational standing of the group, the more items were recorded. Table "A" demonstrates this.

TABLE "A"

MEAN NUMBER OF ITEMS
CORRECTLY RECALLED AND INFERENCES

	Items of Correct Recall			Inferences		
	Law	Police	Settle-ment	Law	Police	Settle-ment
Control	15.2	9.5	5.3	6.8	5.8	4.8
Status-Influence	14.8	13.4	—	10.5	5.8	—
Second Week Only[107]	13.8	9.0	—	7.2	6.2	—
Oral	12.2	8.0	—	5.2	5.6	—
Defense	12.2	—	—	7.1	—	—
Prosecution	15.3	—	—	5.8	—	—
TOTAL	14.0	10.3	5.3	7.2	5.8	4.8

When we discuss means there is, of course, some *overlap* of distribution among groups. There is no sharp line between them. While the mean correct recall for law students was 14.0, the highest single score for a police trainee was 22.0. The highest individual correct recall score for the settlement group was 13.0 which is *higher* than the mean of about 10.0 for the police trainees but *below* the mean for the law students. The highest individual score for a law student was 23.0. This may not seem much better than the highest police trainee's score but there are many more law students who scored in the upper end of the range.

---

[106] This represents a word count of reports made right after film presentation. This, therefore, represents the *maximum* number of words since the word count for the second week is lower. For the Settlement House the word count was based on an English translation for 12 of the 22 subjects who wrote their reports in Spanish— and the reports for 10 subjects who wrote in English. In translation, there was no appreciable difference in word count due to translation.

[107] Second Week Only is average recall a week after the picture was shown. This was the only written report that group wrote. The other means are the averages of reports for both weeks.

This trend of higher correct recall by those people of higher socio-educational status is supported by the mean correct recall of the 10 police trainees who had had some college education. Their mean score was about 14.0, which is significantly different than the mean of the police trainees, although not significantly different from that of the law students. A similar trend is evidenced by the settlement house people. One of them had some college, 9 had some high school, though it was questionable whether more than one had completed high school. Their mean recall score was about 6 whereas those who had only had some elementary schooling scored about 4.

It appears from Table "A" that *not only were there a higher number of items correctly recalled by those of higher educational status, but that there were more inferences, too, by those with more education.* If, however, we compare the proportion of the mean number of inferences to the mean number of items of correct recall, then we find that *the lower the educational status, the greater is the proportion of inferences to items of correct recall.* Whether stated in terms of over-all number of inferences or ratio of inferences to correct recall there would be a considerable degree of inaccuracy in testimony as to the event. The ratio of inferences to correct recall is illustrated by Table "B."

TABLE "B"

RATIO OF MEAN INFERENCE
TO MEAN ITEMS OF CORRECT RECALL[108]

	(N)	Law	(N)	Police	(N)	Settlement
Control	17	44.7%	21	61.0%	22	90.5%
Status-Influence	19	70.9%	22	43.3%	—	—
Second Week Only	19	52.2%	20	68.9%	—	—
Oral	15	42.6%	15	70.0%	—	—
Defense	20	58.2%	—	—	—	—
Prosecution	20	37.9%	—	—	—	—
TOTAL	110[109]	51.4%	78[109]	56.6%	22	90.5%

[108] 100% would mean that there would be an equal number of inferences and correct recall.

[109] Eighty-one other subjects among the law and police groups are not considered here but are considered on pp. 65-66, as they were given different instructions,

In testimony, if inferences are expressed in terms of perception, it is often not possible to distinguish fact from inference. To say, as some did, that the man in the picture was trying to stop the baby from crying, was a statement of recall based on two inferences: the first that there was a baby in the carriage because there was the sound of a baby crying and there was a baby carriage; the second inference built on this was that the man was rocking the baby carriage to quiet the baby. The second inference served to reinforce the first. In each case, the inference was founded on experience that baby carriage + crying baby = the accepted way of quieting a crying baby in a carriage; so, therefore, the man must be trying to quiet a crying baby.[110] In such a situation it cannot be stated as facts that there was a crying baby in the carriage and that the man was trying to quiet it by rocking the carriage.

In addition to correct recall of facts, there was also incorrect recall. The mean number of incorrect items and the ratio of such items to those correctly recalled is shown by Table "C."

TABLE "C"

MEAN NUMBER OF ITEMS INCORRECT ABOUT FACT AND THEIR RATIO TO CORRECT RECALL FOR ALL LAW, POLICE AND SETTLEMENT SUBJECTS FOR BOTH WEEK 1 AND WEEK 2 COMBINED

Mean Number of Incorrect Recall Items		Ratio to Correct Recall Items	
Law	2.8	Law	19.8%
Police	2.5	Police	24.3%
Settlement	1.6	Settlement	31.5%
TOTAL	2.5	TOTAL	21.9%

There were also items recorded which were non-facts, *i.e.*, they were neither correctly nor incorrectly recalled, but stated as facts although not in the picture. It will be seen from Table "D," which gives the mean number of such non-facts and their ratio to facts correctly recalled, that they were not numerous.

---

[110] See Hayakawa, *Meaning, Symbols and Levels of Abstraction*, in NEWCOMB & HARTLEY (eds.), READINGS IN SOCIAL PSYCHOLOGY (1947).

TABLE "D"

MEAN NUMBER OF NON-FACT ITEMS
AND THEIR RATIO TO CORRECT RECALL FOR ALL
LAW, POLICE AND SETTLEMENT SUBJECTS
FOR BOTH WEEK 1 AND WEEK 2 COMBINED

Mean Number of Non-Facts		Ratio to Correct Recall Items	
Law	0.6	Law	4.4%
Police	0.5	Police	4.6%
Settlement	0.2	Settlement	4.3%
TOTAL	0.5	TOTAL	4.5%

Table "E" indicates the ratio of the means of incorrectly recalled facts, non-facts, and inferences taken together to the means of correctly recalled facts for the three populations.

TABLE "E"

MEAN NUMBER OF INCORRECT RECALL ITEMS,
NON-FACT, AND INFERENCES COMBINED
AND THEIR RATIO TO CORRECT RECALL FOR ALL
LAW, POLICE, AND SETTLEMENT SUBJECTS
FOR BOTH WEEK 1 AND WEEK 2 COMBINED

Mean Number of Incorrect Recall, Non-Fact, and Inferences		Ratio to Correct Recall Items	
Law	10.6	Law	75.6%
Police	8.8	Police	85.5%
Settlement	6.6	Settlement	126.3%
TOTAL	9.5	TOTAL	81.4%

This table brings out in stark contrasts the high degree of erroneous "recall" by the three socio-educational groups. This would indicate that a witness may testify to a substantial proportion of "facts" which are not facts at all, and that the lower the socio-educational status of the witness the greater will be the inaccuracy of his testimony, assuming that his testimony is truthful as he perceives truth. It may be, however, that the better educated man will appear more reliable because he can better rationalize his perceptions and express such rationalizations more persuasively. This is brought out in an experiment conducted by Cantril. Six different poems were given to undergraduate students and each had the name of a supposed author. The names of three classical authors, Tennyson,

Keats and Browning were ascribed to poems and the names
of Edgar Guest and two "popular poets," one a "radio poet,"
were also included. All of the poems were by Shakespeare.
The subjects were asked to rank them from 1 to 6, accord-
ing to "literary merit." The "good" poets were ranked
higher than the "poor" poets. A similar experiment with
graduate students in English gave the same result but they
gave "better reasons *why*" the poems were ranked as they
were than did the undergraduates.[111]

Time Elapse

It is not infrequent that the question arises as to the
duration of a happening or how long was the interval between two events. It has been shown that time is difficult
to estimate accurately. (See Chapter I.) A week after
our subjects had seen the picture and after they had made
written or oral reports on their recall, they were asked how
long the picture had taken. Immediately after the picture
was shown, many of them exclaimed, "Is that all!" The
subjects were not under stress when they made their estimates. But we do not usually estimate time while it is passing unless we are prepared to do so, and we rarely are. As
participants in an accident or a crime, or as witnesses, our
attention is not so much fixed on the elapse of time as on
the event. As we shall see in Table "G," action items are
the most frequently recalled. Our perception of the passage
of time is generally a guess after the event. Table "F"
shows the mean estimates made of the picture which had
lasted 42 seconds.

TABLE "F"

MEAN ESTIMATES OF LENGTH OF PICTURE

Law	1 min. 58 sec.
Police	1 min. 28 sec.
Settlement	1 min. 32 sec.

It will be seen that all groups overestimated time and
the law students significantly more than the other two
groups.

[111] Cantril, *Experimental Studies of Prestige Suggestion*, 34 PSY-
CHOLOGY BULL. 528 (1937).

Selectivity

In Chapter I, consideration is given to the phenomenon that perception and recall are selective. This, too, is illustrated by this study, for out of the 115 possible items to be perceived and recalled in the picture that was shown, the highest mean number correctly recalled was 16 by the status-influence group of law students immediately after the picture was shown. A week later in this group the mean number of items correctly recalled had diminished to about 14.

Selectivity also exists among different categories of items. Table "G" indicates the selectivity among items of action, person, background, and sound.

TABLE "G"

FREQUENCY OF CORRECT RECALL OF ITEMS OF ACTION, PERSON, BACKGROUND AND SOUND FOR EACH GROUP AND TOTAL MEANS FOR ALL GROUPS

	Law	Police	Settlement	Total Means
Action	7.29	4.95	2.64	5.91
Background	2.72	2.13	.50	2.25
Sound	2.45	2.16	1.68	2.26
Person	.99	1.09	.45	.96

It will be seen that action items were most frequently recalled by all population groups; and person items least frequently. Background and sound were about the same except for the settlement people who were relatively much better on sound items. The most frequently recalled item was the crying of the baby, which continued throughout most of the film. In action items, it was large movements more than small ones that were most frequently recalled. Thus, in testimony, it would appear that witnesses would be more accurate in describing gross acts and would tend to omit lesser actions, and as a result might distort the probative value of their testimony.

An analysis of the sound items recalled is also instructive with reference to testimony. Two women's voices were heard during the picture; only one of the women could be seen. Both voices were frequently mentioned in the answers, although in a number of cases the substance of what they said was merged and they were heard as if there had been

only one speaker. However, the *content* of what was said
was almost uniformly *inaccurate*. This corroborates the
finding discussed in Chapter I that blanks in perceptions
are filled in by the witness in conformity to his expectations.
As Thucydides said, in reporting speeches, it was necessary
"to make the speaker say what was in my opinion demanded
of them by the various occasions. . . ." [112]

Many a case, of course, turns on the precise language
used in the situation. It would seem that testimony of
precise language is extremely unreliable.

An illustration of such unreliability is dramatized by
replies to questions asked the subjects in a post-questionnaire after they had recorded their recall the week after
they had seen the picture. In the course of the picture, a
woman's voice called out, "Mrs. Gerard, Mrs. Gerard, someone's running away with your baby." A young woman then
ran out of the house shouting, "You bad boy! You bad
boy!" The subjects were asked whether they thought the
woman was the boy's grandmother, mother, a sitter, a
sister, or a neighbor and why they thought so. Seventy
percent of all subjects thought she was the mother. About
a quarter of this three-quarters said that they thought so
because she had said, "My baby." No such words were
used. Another 42% ascribed their conclusion to concern
in voice, to her appearance or age. The other remaining
32% gave a variety of reasons such as "situation," and
what "neighbor" said, etc.

Effect of Direct Questions

Thus, we find that in a situation similar to actual events
testified to at a trial, only a small proportion of facts are
recalled; and that witnesses report a high ratio of errors
of fact, non-facts, and inferences. In a trial there is room
for honest witnesses to differ as to items correctly perceived and recalled. There is also the probability that in
all honesty they will testify as to erroneous perceptions, to
matters that never were but are mistakenly recalled as
perceptions, and to inferences derived from what had actually occurred. Each of these can in good faith be testified to as realities, for to the witness they appear real. As

---

[112] THUCYDIDES, COMPLETE WRITINGS 14 (Modern Library ed.
Crawley transl. 1951).

the result of his experience, they conform to his expectations as to what could or should have been present in the happening.

Because experience has indicated that there are omissions from any perception of what has occurred, lawyers have devised the processes of direct and cross-examination of witnesses to elicit a more complete account, to direct the attention of witnesses to perceptions not immediately recalled.[118] To test the effect of direct questioning after the recital of what had been recalled, a post-questionnaire addressed to specific items in the picture was administered. In other words, having considered free recall, what are the cueing effects of questions which are directed to specific items?

Three questions were asked concerning the appearance of the principal character in the picture. The questions and the summary of the answers follow:

"The man in the picture was dressed in (check one)
a light jacket, dark jacket, wore no jacket."

The correct answer was that he wore a dark jacket. The *direct* question developed more correct recall of this item than the reports, written or spoken, immediately after viewing the picture and one week later, as is shown in Table "H." Most of the written and oral reports contained no mention of the jacket but about 22% of the police trainees described the jacket erroneously. In answer to the direct question, about 50% of the law students and police trainees were in error and 40% of the settlement house people.

TABLE "H"

RESPONSES DESCRIBING JACKET WORN BY PRINCIPAL CHARACTER

| | Free Recall (Written and Oral Reports) | | | Direct Question (Multiple Choice) | |
| | Mentioned | | | | |
	% Correct	% Error	% No Mention	% Correct	% Error
Law	8.0	17.5	75.0	47.4	52.6
Police	6.5	22.5	71.0	49.1	50.9
Settlement	0.0	0.0	100.0	60.0	40.0

[118] We are not considering here the uses of cross-examination to uncover falsity.

Almost no one mentioned in their written or oral reports that the man had sideburns. In answer to the *specific* question on the post-questionnaire, however, about 66% of the law students, about 74% of the police trainees, and 25% of the settlement people reported that he had sideburns. Nevertheless, among the law students, about 19% said he had a mustache and about 4% reported he had a crew cut. The remaining, about 9%, did not answer. For the police trainees these figures were respectively about 23%, 0%, and about 2%. Finally, for the settlement residents they were 35%, 5%, and 35%. It will readily be seen that in spite of better recall under direct presentation of alternatives a substantial number of individuals are either answering wrongly or sufficiently uncertain to make any guess at all. It should be noted that a small percentage of the latter may have omitted the answering due to sheer oversight. But even taking this into account, not much better than approximately two-thirds of all subjects answered correctly on direct questions dealing with what was a perfectly clear and straightforward characteristic of the person in the picture.

The man's race was correctly identified when it was mentioned in the written and oral reports as well as in the answer to a direct question on the post-questionnaire.

A *direct* question in the post-questionnaire relating to action was as to a nonexistent fact. As the picture opened, the principal character lowered the mosquito net on the baby carriage. Nothing was taken out of the baby carriage at any time in the course of the picture. The question was, "At the beginning of the picture did you see the man place his hand in the baby carriage and take something out of it?" If the answer was "Yes," then the question was asked what he took out of the baby carriage and what he did with it. The answers are shown by Table "I."

TABLE "I"

AT THE BEGINNING OF THE PICTURE DID YOU SEE THE MAN PLACE HIS HAND IN THE BABY CARRIAGE AND TAKE SOMETHING OUT OF IT?

	% No	% Yes	% No Answer
Law	85.1	8.0	6.9
Police	78.9	19.3	1.8
Settlement	90.0	5.0	5.0

The striking feature of these responses is the percentage, particularly of police trainees, *who perceived what
had never happened.* These questions and the answers will
be further discussed when consideration is given to the
effect of the status-influence figure.

In answer to the questions what the man had taken
out of the carriage and what he had done with it, those
who had perceived him taking something out replied "a
bottle," "a rattle," or "a mirror." The object was said to
have been put in his pocket, cradled in his arms, shaken,
kept in his hands, put around his neck, etc. This is a clear
case of the witness filling in the gaps in his recollection by
inferences which would sustain his original perception or,
as in this case, misperception.

The answers to these questions bear out Münsterberg's
finding that "As to the influence of questions in the taking
of testimony, the experiments demonstrate that the number of details which the memory produces can certainly be
increased by questions, and, in some cases, even doubled.
But the correctness and exactitude of the testimony de-
creases much more rapidly. This is to a certain degree the
result of the hardly avoidable suggestive character of some
of the questions." [114]

Another action question related to what the woman did
as she came from the house. The post-questionnaire in-
quired whether she was: (a) carrying something in her
hand; (b) waving her left arm with something in her
hand; (c) waving her left arm with nothing in her hand;
or (d) none of these. The correct answer was waving her
left arm with nothing in her hand.

Only one person the first week and two persons the
second, in their written or oral reports, mentioned the
woman waving her hand. In answer to the *direct* question,
however, only 20% of the law students, about 30% of the
police, and 15% of the settlement house people gave the
correct answer. The others either were wrong or made no
response. This might appear to be a reasonable percentage
of correct responses considering the fact that the arm movement was not an essential part of the action of the picture.
However, these percentages of correct recall do not differ
appreciably from what one could expect by chance, that

---

[114] MÜNSTERBERG, PSYCHOLOGY: GENERAL AND APPLIED 401-02
(1915).

is, guessing the answer without even having seen the film, where the guesser has one chance in four of being correct — a 25% chance.

In another question the subjects were directly asked, "How many people's voices did you hear?" Table "J" gives the replies.

TABLE "J"

ANSWERS IN PERCENTAGES TO DIRECT QUESTION ON POST-QUESTIONNAIRE ASKING SUBJECTS, "HOW MANY PEOPLE'S VOICES DID YOU HEAR?"

	1 Voice	2 Voices	3 Voices	"Unclear"	No Answer
Law	29.1%	46.8%	13.7%	3.6%	6.8%
Police	28.1%	49.1%	14.9%	0.0%	7.9%
Settlement	15.0%	20.0%	30.0%	0.0%	35.0%

There were three voices—a crying baby and two women. It will be seen from Table "J" that less than one-fifth of the subjects heard correctly, except in the case of the settlement house people, 30% of whom heard three voices. While it might have been difficult for some to distinguish between the voice that called, "Mrs. Gerard, Mrs. Gerard, quick! Someone's running away with your baby" and the voice of the woman coming from the house who shouted, "You bad boy! You bad boy!", which might lead to the inference by some that there was only one woman's voice, in view of the almost continuous crying of a baby (the most recalled item of all), the answer "one" voice was patently wrong. It is possible that there was semantic difficulty and that to some a baby's cry is not a "people's voice. In a trial, this might have been cleared up by further direct questioning. It evidences a value of direct and cross-examination. However, in view of the answers to a subsequent question as to who the woman coming from the house was and the fact that about 63% of the law students answering the question, and about 80% of the police trainees answering the question, and 85% of the settlement house people answering the question said that the woman was the mother, it would indicate that the voices were distinguished but not recalled as separate voices (see discussion p. 54). This is a condensation, a merging process, "as though memory tries to burden itself as little as possible. For instance, instead of remembering two items, it is more economical to fuse them into one." [115]

The baby carriage was almost continuously in view; nevertheless, about 10% of the answers of all subjects to the *direct* question whether the hood was up or down or whether there was no hood were in error. The error for the law group was about 12%, for police about 8%, and for the settlement house about 11%. This was considered a background item (*i.e.*, neither action, personal, nor sound).

Another *direct* question concerning background was, "How many doors were there in the house?" And this was followed up by questions as to the difference between the doors, and whether they saw the woman go out of a door and, if so, which one. The correct answer was two doors, which was given by about 17% of the law students, about 32% of the police trainees, and 5% of the settlement house people. Here the police trainees scored notably higher than the others, but still only about one-third perceived the correct number of doors. (In the written and oral replies made immediately after the picture was shown and a week later, only one door was mentioned by 19% of the law students, 26% by the police trainees, and 6% by the settlement house people.) Thus, it will be seen that the police trainees did best, especially under direct questioning. Yet, only about 32% of the police trainees were accurate and about 67% were in error, which is not significantly better than would be expected by chance.

Status-Influence

What effect does status-influence have on recall? A witness is almost always affected by status-influence at some stage of trial. To many prospective witnesses the person who interviews them before they go on the stand is such a status figure. To almost all people a prosecuting attorney is, and it is a reasonable supposition that to all witnesses the judge at the trial has status-influence which affects them if for no other reason than that his status involves power. That is, he has the power to give approval which may be rewarding, and he has punitive power which may be threatening. Fromm suggests that "Even the picture of the judge, who, in democratic society, is elected and

---

[115] Allport & Postman, *op. cit. supra* note 69, at 64.

theoretically not above his fellow men, is tinged by the old concept of a judging god. Although his person does not carry any superhuman power, his office does. (The forms of respect due the judge are surviving remnants of the respect due a superhuman authority; contempt of court is psychologically closely related to *lèse-majesté*.)" [116] A judge's influence may also derive from his possible status as a reference figure, that is, a model to whose views and behavior another person attempts to adapt himself.

Immediately after showing the picture the experimenters asked a group of law students to go to a separate room with their law professor, and a group of police trainees to do the same with one of their instructors who was a police captain who wore his uniform for the occasion, although generally he did not do so in the Police Academy. In both instances, the experimenters delayed going into the room to administer their questionnaires until the status figure, *i.e.*, the professor or the police captain, made the following statement:

> "It is extremely important that each of you gives us as much of his recollection as he possibly can, both as to what he heard and saw. I am particularly anxious that you do well in this. Very often it is found that the people answering the questionnaire omit simple things which may be important in a trial. For example, there was a tree on the lawn in front of the house. Or that at the very beginning the man put his hand in the carriage and took something out. Or in describing the house that the door on the right was partly open, or that the man, at the end, squatted under a mail box. It is all this kind of detail that we would like to have from you in so far as you can recall what you saw and heard."

A few minutes later an experimenter entered the room to distribute questionnaires. He did not remain in the room but the status figure did. The second week these (the status) groups remained in the same room with the other subjects to fill out their second questionnaires on their recall and the separate post-questionnaire.

No significant effect of status-influence was found in inducing recollection of the specific items or recording the non-facts mentioned by the status figure. However, as is

---

[116] FROMM, MAN FOR HIMSELF 235 (1947).

shown by Table "K," the word count, the recall of facts, and the number of inferences were markedly affected and significantly different.

TABLE "K"

MEAN WORD COUNT, CORRECT RECALL AND INFERENCES FOR STATUS-INFLUENCE CONDITION IN LAW AND POLICE GROUPS AS COMPARED TO THEIR CONTROL GROUPS

Word Count	Control	Status
Law	183	264
Police	135	178

Correct Recall	Control	Status
Law	15.2	14.8
Police	9.5	13.4

Inferences	Control	Status
Law	6.8	10.5
Police	5.8	5.8

Correct Recall and Inferences	Control	Status
Law	22.0	25.3
Police	15.3	19.2

It will be seen that for both law students and police trainees the effect of the status-influence person resulted in longer written reports. The effect of the status-influence person differed, however, with respect to each of the two groups: (1) the law student status-influence group made more inferences than did any other law or police group; and (2) the police trainee status-influence group had better recall than any other police group. (See Table "A.") As will be seen in Table "B" the ratio of inferences to correct recall was about 71% for the law students and about 43% for the police trainees in the status-influence condition.

The subjects in the status-influence condition had the same perceptual opportunity as those in the other conditions and each population group studied was of a different socio-educational status than the others. *This would imply that the quantity of matter recalled by a witness, the correctness of his recall and the proportion of his testimony that is inferential are dependent upon influences of others on him (not necessarily intentional influences), as well as upon his perception, his socio-educational status or other variables.*

Oral Reporting

Witnesses are rarely called to the stand without having previously made a statement, oral or in writing, to an attorney or investigator. It would appear that a written statement would bring out better recall.

This is borne out by Table "A" which reveals that those who reported orally as to what they had seen and heard recalled less and made fewer inferences than those who *wrote* their reports. (However, the law school group who were told they were for the defense were no different from the oral group in their recall.) When we consider the ratio of inferences to recall in the oral group (Figure 1), we find it to be about 70% for the police trainees and about 42% for the law students.

Furthermore, the question arises as to the reliability of recall by jurors in the jury room whose deliberations involve their oral restatement of the testimony to which they were witnesses. This might well be worthy of further research.

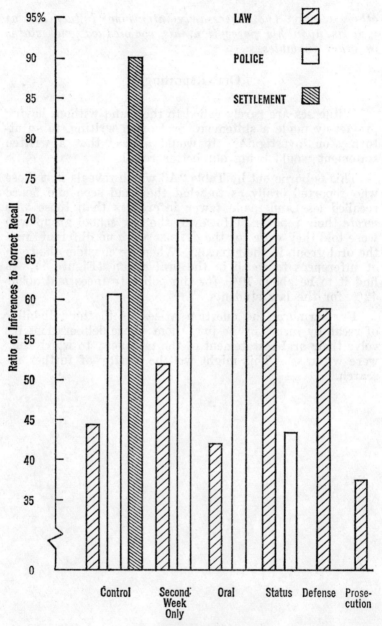

Figure 1. Ratio of Inferences to Correct Recall in Each Experimental Condition for Law, Police, and Settlement Groups.

In the case of the oral groups, there was some delay in the administration of the questionnaires before the subjects reported on tape. The first week the law students had to leave the hall where the picture was shown and go to another building, where they made their recordings in two shifts, the second shift more than half an hour after the picture was shown. The police trainees went to a different floor of the Police Academy and took turns using four recording instruments, which were all that were available. This meant a considerable delay before their recordings were completed. In both instances this delay might account for the lower percentage of correct recall in the oral than in the written reports.

Bias

It has been found that perception and recall are also dependent on the *bias* of the observer. Bias may determine attitude, which is similar to expectation in that it is a readiness for reinforcement. In this experiment, bias was introduced by informing half the subjects that the man in the picture who had been indicted for attempted kidnapping had previously been twice convicted for molesting children. No statistically reliable difference was found between the subjects who were given this biasing information and those who were not, either in the amount of correct recall or inferences made. This does not prove that bias has no effect on recall, but may mean only that the biasing information given in this experiment was ineffective.

However, although most of the subjects were informed that the principal character had been indicted, and that they would be called as witnesses, one group of 20 law students did not get this information. They had the highest correct recall of any of the law student groups (a mean of 16.10 items) and the lowest number of inferences (a mean of 4.90 items).[117] The difference cannot be dependent on the fact that they were not told they would be witnesses, because that variable was applied to other subjects and showed no statistically reliable effect. Was it then that not telling these subjects that the principal character was indicted caused them to feel no need to "take sides" and

---

[117] A similar group of police trainees was too small to be statistically significant.

resulted in less stress? Does conscious or unconscious commitment to a party to litigation, or involvement in a process of fixing responsibility, placing blame, tend to reduce correct recall? Or does the mere fact of receiving no extraneous information enable one to recall more of a happening?

The result appears different, however, when there is reason to believe that the accused is *unsound mentally*. A group of 20 law students was given this bias by being informed that the principal character had been indicted for attempted kidnapping and that he "has a history of mental illness." Their mean correct recall was about 11%, the lowest of any of the law groups and their mean inferences were about 7%.[118] (Compare these figures to Table "A.")

Inferring from the fact that a person had been in a mental institution that he was a "mental case," the conclusion would follow that he was not fully responsible for his behavior and therefore did not intend to kidnap. As Heider said, ". . . if we are convinced that *o* did *x* intentionally we generally link the *x* more intimately with the person than if we think that *o* did *x* unintentionally. By the same token, if we account for an act by a person's stupidity or clumsiness, that is, by ability factors, we tend to hold him less responsible than if we take the act as an indication of his motives."[119]

In such circumstances, facts which might or might not be felt to be relevant to inducing punitive action, such as holding a normal person responsible for his behavior, might appear irrelevant and be discarded if it was believed that the actor was after all a "mental case." To many people, moreover, mental illness is threatening to them and they would tend to avoid facts which they might feel would be descriptive of what they themselves might do.

Effect of Time on Recall

The decline in material recalled after a lapse of time, the slippage of memory, has already been discussed in Chapter I. As a result of the selective process, as has been shown, only a small proportion of the happenings were re-

---

[118] While a similar group of police trainees indicated the same trend as to correct recall, their number was too small to be statistically significant.

[119] HEIDER, THE PSYCHOLOGY OF INTERPERSONAL RELATIONS 112 (1958).

called immediately after viewing the picture. The decline or slippage of memory was not as great the following week. Perhaps the process of leveling and sharpening had slowed down. It would be interesting to know how much memory remained after one month or a year and whether over such greater intervals of time the rate of reduction would have increased or whether it had approached a point of decline at which the rate of change would become smaller and smaller. With one exception inferences also decreased. Would they have decreased further or increased with a greater lapse of time? We do not have the data to determine this.

Time elapse, however, between an occurrence and the need to recall it is only one factor in this phenomenon of forgetting. "For 'time' alone does not cause the forgetting . . . ." [120] Table "L" and Figure 2 not only show the deterioration of memory after one week but also indicate how *people differ in their recall under varied conditions.* What happens is a process of leveling, sharpening, and assimilation which occurs not only in the progress of rumor but also in "the individual memory function as well." [121]

There is also a reduction in the number of inferences after the lapse of a week.

---

[120] Levine & Murphy, *The Learning and Forgetting of Controversial Material,* in READINGS IN SOCIAL PSYCHOLOGY 100 (Maccoby, Newcomb & Hartley 3d ed. 1958).

[121] Allport & Postman, *The Basic Psychology of Rumor,* in READINGS IN SOCIAL PSYCHOLOGY 64 (Maccoby, Newcomb & Hartley 3d ed. 1958).

TABLE "L"

MEAN NUMBER OF ITEMS OF CORRECT RECALL AND INFERENCES FIRST AND SECOND WEEKS

| | Correct Recall | | | | | | Inferences | | | | | |
| | Law | | Police | | Settlement | | Law | | Police | | Settlement | |
	W1	W2	W1	W2	W1	W2	W1	W2	W1	W2	W1	W2
Control	16.2	14.3	10.0	9.0	5.4	5.1	7.1	6.5	7.3	4.2	4.6	4.9
Status	16.0	13.5	13.8	13.0			12.0	9.0	6.7	5.0		
Week 2 only*		13.8		9.0				7.2		6.2		
Oral	12.4	11.9	8.1	7.9			5.6	4.9	6.2	5.1		
Defense	12.6	11.6					7.2	7.0				
Prosecution	15.9	14.7					6.4	5.3				
TOTAL	14.7	13.2	10.9	10.2	5.4	5.1	7.7	6.6	6.8	4.8	4.6	4.9

* Second Week Only: These groups only reported one week after seeing the picture.

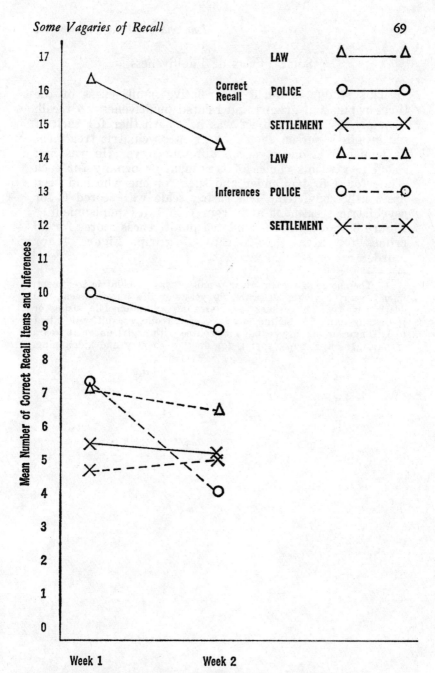

Figure 2. Mean Number of Correct Recall Items and Inferences During Week 1 and Week 2 for the Control Conditions in Each of the Law, Police, and Settlement Groups.

Some Effects of Punitiveness

This study examined the relative punitiveness of the three population groups and related punitiveness to recall. In a pre-test each subject was asked whether for each of ten crimes a person should be given psychiatric treatment or punished in one of seven different ways. He was first asked to give his choice of treatment or penalty for each crime for a first offender and then for one who had been previously convicted. The rating scale was scored 0 for psychiatric treatment and from 1 to 7 for punishment.[122] Figure 3 shows the consolidated punitiveness scores for all crimes for each socio-educational group, Figure 4 for murder.

---

[122] The choice of treatment or penalties was psychiatric treatment, fine, 1 year, 5 years, 10 years, 20 years or life imprisonment and death penalty. The crimes were stealing an automobile, using or possessing narcotics, selling any type of narcotic, assault with intent to kill, murder, having sexual intercourse with a girl under 16 years of age, gambling, rape, spying for another country and kidnapping.

Punishments for Ten Crimes

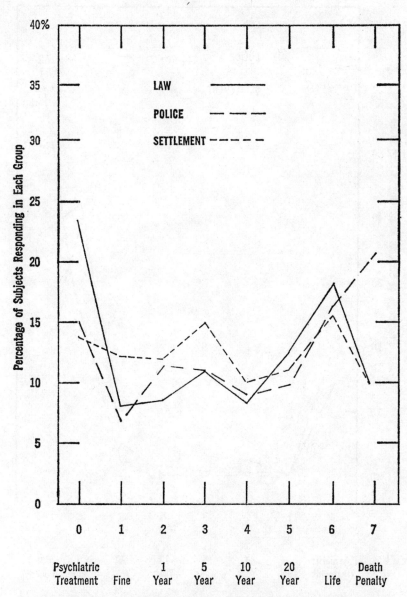

Figure 3. The Means of Responses to All Ten Crimes Expressed in Percentages for Each Punishment Category in the Law, Police, and Settlement Groups.

Punishments for Murder

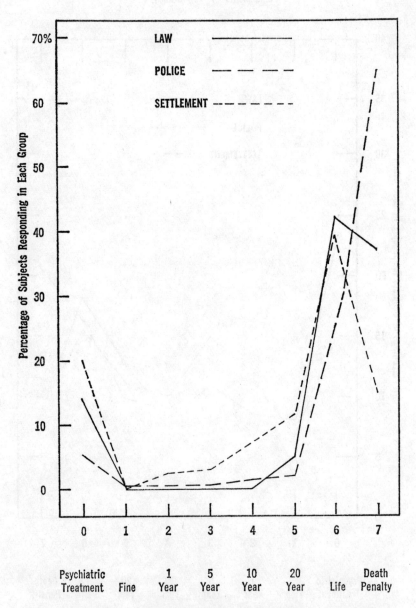

Figure 4. The Means of Responses to *Murder* Expressed in Percentages for Each Punishment Category in the Law, Police, and Settlement Groups.

The consolidated scores for all ten crimes indicate the following three most prevalent dispositions by each population group:

Law Students:

    18.6% for life imprisonment
    12.4% for 20 years imprisonment
    23.2% for psychiatric treatment

Police Trainees:

    17.0% for life imprisonment
    20.6% for death
    15.2% for psychiatric treatment

Settlement House:

    16.4% for life imprisonment
    14.8% for five years imprisonment
    14.3% for psychiatric treatment

Thus the death penalty was not one of the three most favored choices of the law students or settlement house people, but the most frequent choice of penalty (over one-fifth) by the police trainees.

Choice for each population group of a fine as punishment was:

Law Students	8.0%
Police Trainees	6.4%
Settlement House	12.0%

It will be noted that the settlement house people chose a fine more frequently than either of the two other population groups. We have no data to explain this. Possibly it was, because of their economic position, a fine seemed more serious to them; or they may have deemed the crimes for which they selected a fine less serious; or they might have been less punitive and concentrated more on the lower end of the scale.

Figure 4 dramatizes the differences in punitiveness among the three groups. It refers only to the punishments

they would give for *murder*. Sixty-five percent of the police
would give the death penalty as compared to about 41%
of the law students and 17% of the settlement house people.

The median on the punitive scale (from 0 to 7) for
the law students was 3.41, for the police trainees 4.00, and
for the settlement house people 3.39. It will be seen that
the police trainees emerge with significantly higher scores
on the punitive scale than the law students and settlement
house people. The latter two groups do not differ from
each other significantly.

The median split for punitiveness, combining all three
groups, is 3.69. The percentage of each group above and
below the combined median for punitiveness is shown in
Table "M."

TABLE "M"

PERCENTAGE OF SUBJECTS IN EACH OF LAW, POLICE, AND SETTLEMENT GROUPS FALLING ABOVE AND BELOW THE MEDIAN ON PUNITIVE SCALE FOR ALL SUBJECTS TAKEN TOGETHER

	High Punitive	Low Punitive	Total Percent
Law	40.9%	59.1%	100.00
Police	67.3%	32.7%	100.00
Settlement	31.9%	68.1%	100.00

It appears clearly that about two thirds of the police trainees
rank above the combined population punitive median and
that the law students and settlement house people are relatively low. In other words, counting people in each group
we find that the police trainees distribute themselves much
more on the high end of the scale measuring "punitiveness."

Dividing each population group into high and low punitive (the high being above the median for each population,
the low below the median on the ten crimes), it was found
that *the above median subjects of each population had
higher scores of correct recall than did the low punitive.*
They also had higher scores for incorrect recall and lower
scores for inferences, though neither of these was statistically significant. A comparison of the recall of high
and low punitive subjects appears in Table "N."

TABLE "N"

PUNITIVENESS EFFECTS ON CORRECT RECALL
(SEPARATE MEDIANS FOR EACH GROUP)

	Punitive Groups High	Low
Law	14.86	13.86
Police	11.83	9.86
Settlement	6.73	3.82
TOTAL	12.53	10.84

It is apparent that two independent variables affecting recall are present. While the mean recall of each socio-educational group is as shown in Table "A," *supra*, that is, the law students having best recall, then the police trainees and then the settlement house people, *within each socio-educational group, there is a significant difference between the high and low punitive in correct recall.*

The data of this experiment do not answer conclusively whether the greater punitiveness on the part of the police is due to a selective process by which men choosing police work tend to be more punitive, or more punitive applicants are selected as better fitting the model of what a policeman should be, or whether even after a short period in the Police Academy the trainees have adapted to a stereotype of a role which pictures a policeman as severe, hardboiled, and punitive. Selectivity and role may both be involved.

The police trainees showed *greater rigidity, i.e.,* unwillingness to lean backwards, than did the other populations studied. In answer to a question on the pre-questionnaire as to whether they would tend to lean backwards in a case where the penalty was more severe than where it was less severe, only 37% of the police trainees said yes, whereas 50% of the law students and 52% of the settlement house people replied in the affirmative. Again, whether this is the result of a selection process or role adaptation is uncertain.

Rigidity is one of the characteristics of the authoritarian personality. Another such personality characteristic is the response to authority.[123] The different effects of authority

---

[123] ADORNO, FRENKEL-BRUNSWICK, LEVINSON & SANFORD, THE AUTHORITARIAN PERSONALITY (The American Jewish Comm., Studies in Prejudice Series: Pub. No. 3, 1950).

on law students and police trainees appear in Table "K." The status-influence figure (a professor in the case of the law students and a police captain in uniform in the case of the police trainees) had the effect of producing half as many inferences by the police trainees as by the law students. The former, in response to the status figure's instructions, gave more correct facts than their control group and the same number of inferences, whereas there were no statistically different numbers of facts and substantially more inferences reported by the law school status-influence group than by their control group.

The answers to another question suggest the adaptation of police trainees to the policeman's role. This question was asked:

> "Suppose that a trusted employee steals money from his employer on Monday. On Friday he returns the money and is caught when doing so. In your opinion, which of the following actions should be taken by the employer?"

Five answers were proposed and the subjects were asked to check one. The answers were:

> "(1) Say nothing and forget the matter; (2) Bawl out the employee but do nothing further; (3) Transfer the employee to a job where he can't get his hands on money; (4) Report the matter to the police; or (5) Report the matter to the police and insist on prosecution."

Seventy-five percent of the law students, 79% of the settlement house people, and only 58% of the police trainees answered (2) or (3). However, 35% of the police checked answer (4) ("Report the matter to the police") compared to 8.8% of the law students and 9% of the settlement house people.

Another question revealed attitude differences between the law students and police trainees. They were asked:

> "The law says that a person accused of a crime should be considered innocent until proven guilty. Still, it is said that where there is smoke there is likely to be some fire. It would probably be better, therefore, to assume that a person who is accused is likely to be guilty, but to give him the benefit of the doubt by adjusting the severity of the punishment. If there is

some doubt, give him the mildest punishment possible for that crime. If there is no doubt about his guilt, give him the most severe punishment that the law prescribes for that crime.

"To what extent do you agree or disagree with the above statement? (Check one answer only.)

"(1) Agree very strongly; (2) Agree somewhat; (3) Can't decide; (4) Disagree somewhat; or (5) Disagree very strongly."

Eighty-two percent of the law students replied: "Disagree very strongly," but only 44% of the police trainees gave this response and 25% of them said either that they agreed very strongly or agreed somewhat, compared to less than 1% of the law students. (As 38% of the settlement house people answered, "Can't decide," it appeared that the question probably was too difficult for them and so their replies are not considered here.) This too may be a case of adaptation to the expectations of role, the law students accepting the principle of Anglo-American law that a man is innocent until proven guilty and a large proportion of the police trainees suspecting the accused and preferring to give him some punishment if there is doubt as to his guilt. "Since the police officer obtains his rewards and satisfactions from the successful identification of persons responsible for misconduct, and since such success is 'confirmed' through prosecution, conviction and sentencing, any interference with this sequence may be experienced as terribly frustrating." [124]

---

[124] Toch, *Psychological Consequences of the Police Role*, a paper presented at the Annual Meeting of the American Psychological Association, September 1, 1963. See also Allport & Postman, *The Basic Psychology of Rumor*, in READINGS IN SOCIAL PSYCHOLOGY 54, 63, 65 (Maccoby, Newcomb & Hartley 3d ed. 1958). They showed to a group of police officers a picture involving police and a night stick. In the account of the picture by the police officers, "The entire reproduction centered around the police officer (with whom the subjects undoubtedly felt keen sympathy or 'identification'). Furthermore, the night stick, a symbol of their power, . . . becomes the main object of the controversy. The tale as a whole is protective of, and partial to, the policeman." This reaction is, of course, not peculiar to the police. Allport and Postman mention a picture "containing women's dresses, as a trifling detail," which in the telling became "a story exclusively about dresses."

As policemen are frequently witnesses, the quality of
their testimony is important. Their greater tendency toward punitiveness than that of the other two population
groups referred to and their greater rigidity have been
mentioned. Toch and Schulte found that advance police
administration students *perceive more violence* in a situation than do first-year police administration students or
students in their first year of psychology. In their experiment, Toch and Schulte showed their subjects nine stereo-
grams which simultaneously presented to one eye a picture
of a crime being committed (violence) and to the other a
neutral picture. The advance students saw twice as many
violent pictures as did the first-year police students and
more than twice as many as the psychology students. Toch
and Schulte say that, "Given a task in which others pre-
dominantly perceive non-violent content, subjects with police schooling have become relatively aware of violent content." "This does not mean," they tell us, "that the law
enforcer necessarily comes to exaggerate the prevalence of
violence. It means that the law enforcer may come to accept crime *as a familiar personal experience*, one which he
himself is not surprised to encounter. The acceptance of
crime as a familiar experience in turn increases the *ability*
or readiness to perceive violence where clues to it are po-
tentially available." [125] It may, however, be another function
of punitiveness.

*Why do the more punitive people have greater correct
recall?* Freyberg investigated a series of "variables that
enter into interpersonal decision-making and that may lead
to the perception that another desires to increase his power
in a relationship." He suggests that the subjects of his
experiment had greater recall of the arguments of another
person who was pitted against them when they "had
grounds for suspecting the veracity of *C*'s [the other person's] expressed opinions." [126] This would mean that if the
more punitive people felt their sense of power threatened
they would be more alert to threatening situations, that
their sensitivity to their environment and to happenings
would be sharpened.

---

[125] Toch & Schulte, *Readiness To Perceive Violence as a Result
of Police Training*, 52, 4 BRITISH J. PSYCHOLOGY 389, 391-92 (1961).

[126] Freyberg, *The Effect of Mistrust in Interpersonal Decision-
Making on Hostility* (unpublished Doctoral Dissertation, Grad. School
of Arts and Science, N.Y.U. (1962)).

It would seem that people who are extra-punitive would tend to look outside of themselves for cues, because they would want to place the blame outside of themselves and not look into their own punitiveness, whereas people who are intra-punitive would look for blame in themselves as well as outside. This would consume more energy and therefore would leave them less energy to pursue the extraneous facts than that available to the extra-punitive persons.

Extra-punitiveness can be conceived as a projection of one's own faults and weaknesses on to others. This would require the extra-punitive to look outward for situations appropriate to such projection, situations in which they could safely project faults and weaknesses on to others without invoking punitive authority towards themselves. Responding to persons with status-influence or testifying for the prosecution or prescribing severe punishments for social deviants might be appropriate situations. Thus the extra-punitive are in greater need than the intra-punitive to have information about their environment to determine (mostly unconsciously) when they can safely reduce the tensions of their motives without exposing themselves to retribution.[126a]

These findings concerning punitiveness do not mean that in all situations these socio-educational groups would show the same relative punitiveness or hostility. It is probable that punitiveness is a function of situation as well as socio-educational status. In other words, if other questions had been put to them the settlement house people might have proven more punitive, but they were less punitive in considering punishments which the law might inflict because of their own frequent involvement with the law. It is clear that they have more trouble with the police, for example, than do the other groups of the population.[127]

Table "O" shows the replies to the question: "What experience have you had with the police that you think was fair or unfair? Please write below what this experience was."

[126a] ADORNO, FRENKEL-BRUNSWICK, LEVINSON & SANFORD, *op. cit. supra* note 123, at 409-11; SARNOFF, PERSONALITY DYNAMICS AND DEVELOPMENT 150 (1962).

[127] And the police have different attitudes toward them than to middle-class people. Toch, *Psychological Consequences of the Police Role, supra* note 124.

TABLE "O"

"UNFAIR," "FAIR," AND "NOT ANSWERED" EXPERIENCES WITH POLICE

	N	X	%	X	%	X	%
	Unfair			Fair		No Answer	
Law	184	30	16.3	17	9.2	137	74.5
Police	125	6	4.8	9	7.2	110	88.0
Settlement	51	15	29.4	3	5.9	33	64.7

N = Number Subjects Overall

X = Number of Subjects in the Category

% = Percent of Subjects in the Category of Over-all (Total) Number

It is clear that the settlement house people have the most complaints, more than the law students and the police trainees. The complaints are significantly different from each other. One of the police trainees criticized the police with the entertaining account of the following incident:

> "I once found something (a wallet) and turned it in to the police precinct. They did not even thank me. I was rather annoyed."

Most of the law students' complaints dealt with traffic tickets although one law student complained of illegal searches by the police of all teen-agers in the neighborhood "just because it had a high delinquency rate." The settlement house people, on the other hand, had more serious complaints, such as the following:

> "On one occasion two detectives impounded my husband's automobile without any reason or proof. They claimed that he was selling dope (pusher) and narcotics. After an argument of several minutes the detectives withdrew because they could not find anything that would justify their insinuations [charge]. This was natural and to be expected because my husband is a man who never had problems before with the police. He always lived honorably from his work. I thought this was a scandal—and our neighbors intruded themselves into this and caused us great humiliation. The police barged into our house and humiliated us in front of the neighbors."

There are certain related trends apparent in this data: high punitive people and those assuming the role of witnesses for the prosecution have greater correct recall than do low punitive people, people assuming the role of witness for the defendant, and those who believe that an indicted defendant is mentally ill. It would appear, then, that the high punitive people and witnesses for the prosecution are more aggressively motivated than the others. This would indicate that recall is a function of aggressive motivation, at least within each socio-educational population group.

Just as we have no data indicating a relationship between intelligence and correct recall, so, too, our data does not indicate that there is a difference in intelligence between high and low punitive people, though the former have better correct recall.

In summary, where there is a greater verbal capacity, there is greater correct recall and there are a greater number of inferences but a lower ratio of inferences to correct recall. Within each socio-educational group, where there is high punitiveness, there is greater recall and less where there is low punitiveness. When a status figure urges subjects to do well there is a greater number of inferences by law students and less by the police trainees than by their control groups. Among the law students, those who were told that they would be witnesses for the prosecution had greater recall than those who were told that they would be witnesses for the defendants. (See Tables "A," "B," and "L.")

For the trial lawyer and the court this would imply that the accuracy of recall does not stand alone but is related to such variables as socio-educational status, role, and personality factors, such as punitiveness. At the present state of the law, there is little that a trial court can do to relate accuracy of recall to those variables. Do these phenomena not, however, present a challenge to lawyers and judges to stimulate and participate in research to test new judicial practices that might produce greater objective reality in testimony, that might produce greater correspondence between what is perceived and recalled by those who testify (their subjective reality) and what is objectively real? Do we not need to be able to identify those factors that bear upon differences in the recall of witnesses for the plaintiff or prosecution and for the defendant, and witnesses who react differently to various influences?

CHAPTER III

IN THE COURTROOM

Advocacy as a Change Process

Thus far we have been considering principally perception, recollection, and articulation as they affect a witness to a happening or event. We have discussed the relativity of reality in such transactions and the "As If" assumption of some of the rules of evidence. Now we shall focus on the psychological transactions and inter-relationships of advocacy and fact-finding, the attorneys and the judge and jury.

The lawyer's concern with reality is not only with fact but also effect. He must evaluate evidence in terms of how it will appear to the judge and jury. Normally in contract negotiation or in litigation there is a play for position. That is part of the game. But the successful lawyer, however just he may deem his cause or with whatever assurance he may present it, cannot afford to indulge in psychological *denial* of *facts*, disagreeable, incongruent facts, which may be presented by his opponent. He cannot afford to close his mind to the *interpretations* his opponent might offer in the course of his advocacy. A lawyer or negotiator must also constantly be aware of how *his* reality will appear not only to his opponent but to such neutrals as the judge and jury.

This is a different aspect of the problem of reality from that which is described by the testimony. The appearance of a piece of evidence to the judge and jury is a product of their expectations, experiences, belief systems, and sympathies, which make reality for them. Within the "As If" system of the law, the ultimate test of reality to the lawyer is: will a witness or a piece of evidence succeed in moving the triers of fact to a response favorable to his case? Consequently, the manner in which evidence is presented may be to the trial counsel as important as the facts themselves. This is at least tacitly recognized in Great Britain, where the solicitor gathers the facts and the barrister presents them. It is increasingly common in this country, too, for special trial counsel to be retained.

The Change Process

The lawyer trying a case has the task of bringing about *change*. He must bring the attitude of judge and jury from neutrality or hostility to supportiveness. One effective way to bring about change is to involve the person or persons to be changed in the process of planning and installing the change.[128] It is scarcely feasible for judge and jury to be involved in such a self-changing process—at least within the law and our prevailing ethical principles. They can, however, be involved emotionally by stimulation in them of a tension, a need, a motive to change their attitudes to favorable ones. Consequently, theories of change become relevant.

When we are in conflict over some contradiction, some dissonant concepts, some ambivalence or imbalance of feeling, as in the case of conflicting evidence, we try to resolve it. We may attempt to eliminate conflict by ceasing to think about it, that is, we try to deny that the conflicting evidence exists. Counsel may attempt to get the jury to forget about an item of evidence by ignoring it or belittling it so that it appears irrelevant, unworthy of consideration or contradictory to other more credible evidence. If we feel that a piece of evidence really has little or no value, then we are relieved of whatever conflict it has caused.

Usually, however, counsel will attempt resolution by differentiation. For example, fifty miles an hour may have been the lawful speed limit but in this case the defendant was passing a truck and it was negligence not to have a clear view before making the attempt. This was, then, a different situation than one in which fifty miles an hour would be legitimate, reasonable. The attorney does the same thing in arguing the law. The case of *A v. B* is irrelevant, he points out, because although in that case the facts *X* and *F* were present, here fact *Z* makes the case different. "So with the growth of law. The judge stretches a point here in response to a moral urge, or makes a new applica-

---

[128] Coch & French, Jr., *Overcoming Resistance to Change*, 1 HUMAN RELATIONS 512-32 (1948).

tion of a precedent there. Before long a new tradition has arisen. . . . The moral norm and the jural have been brought together, and are one." [128a] Differentiation is our common response to conflict pressures and therefore is an easy technique for the attorney and an acceptable one to court and jury.

This process of differentiation may not merely resolve a conflict, remove a block to the acceptance by the jury of counsel's case, it may at times change their attitude. For example, if it can be made to appear that the plaintiff was not just reckless in running to the middle of the highway but was trying to save a dog, the attitude of the jury may be changed from a negative to a positive one: the plaintiff was a hero.

Of course, the most effective way to change attitudes, to reduce dissonance or ambivalence, is to bring added social support to reinforce acceptance of the desired change or resolution. The degree of social support that a concept yields is related to the source of the concept. If we like or admire someone we tend to accept his ideas; and we reject them if we dislike or despise him. To a lesser extent, disliked ideas may reduce the lustre of an otherwise admired source and make him unacceptable, and vice versa. [129] In social research itself the acceptability of the experimenter appears to be a variable, the more admired experimenter seemingly being able to effect greater change in behavior. [130]

Counsel himself may be so acceptable to the jury that his words alone can give to a juryman the support necessary to reduce his conflict and change his attitude. But usually support in resolving conflict within the triers of fact is provided by presenting the evidence in such a way that doubtful testimony is reinforced by a succession of corroborating witnesses, examples from common experience, or, perhaps, documents and photographs.

[128a] CARDOZO, THE PARADOXES OF LEGAL SCIENCE 43 (1928), referring to VAIHINGER, DIE PHILOSOPHIE DES ALS OB [THE PHILOSOPHY OF THE "AS IF"] (Ogden transl. 1935).

[129] Brown, *Models of Attitude Change*, in BROWN, GALANTIER, HESS & MANDLER, NEW DIRECTIONS IN PSYCHOLOGY 1, 38 (Barron ed. 1962). The application of these models of attitude change, discussed by Brown, to the process of the law would appear to be a worthwhile area for research.

[130] *Id.* at 39.

Counsel wants to be accepted by judge and jury. He
wants to win their support as a means to winning their
judgment or verdict in his favor. Styles in the conduct
of a case may differ and one attorney will be more sensi-
tive to feedback from his interaction with judge and jury
than another. Some, poor souls, can never appear as other
than pettifoggers. By gaining acceptance from judge and
jury, counsel not only gains their support but is in a position to support them in some attitude favorable to his case.

Having established his own acceptability, perhaps in
the course of doing so, he then must build up his client
and witnesses and if possible reduce the acceptability of
the opposing parties and witnesses, so that in the scale of
social acceptance his side will generate greater acceptance
than the other. We could put this in another way: If a
lawyer can achieve greater balance for his side of the case,
then this will be supportive of jury and judge who render
a verdict or judgment in his favor. They need support
from him in return for meeting his need for their support. This support he provides them when he can make
his case appear more reasonable to them, more consonant
with their values, than his opponent's.

Values arise from expectations and so there is the tendency to accept what is expected of a situation. It is this
that makes evidence credible, meeting the values or norms
of judge and jury because it satisfies their expectations;
or conversely it meets their expectations because it satisfies
their values or norms. To make behavior appear normal,
even the absurd reasonable, is an accepted problem of advocacy.

A trial lawyer is probably most successful if he intro-
duces the contradictions, inaccuracies, or falsifications of
the opposing witnesses, or the weakness of his opponent's
interpretation, after he has established a supportive relationship between himself and the jury. In his advocacy
the lawyer is not unlike the salesman who only after he
"has established himself as a man of good taste . . . can
venture some esteem capital by speaking out for a sofa
whose costliness renders it mildly negative for the customer
and hope to draw that sofa sufficiently high on the value
scale to bring it across the purchase threshold." [131]

This is well understood by trial lawyers. The good will,
the acceptance earned by counsel is an investment in his

---

[131] Brown, *op. cit. supra* note 129, at 37.

cause. It makes possible a positive identification of himself with his client. For example, Gair says:

> "We must make full use of the psychological principle of identification: identification in the eyes of the jury between you and your client, and identification of the jury with what has befallen your client." [132]

It is often believed that such psychological approaches are not important in presenting cases to judges. Perhaps not. It would be interesting to find empirical evidence as to this belief. In any event, experienced trial lawyers do not believe that judges are immune from similar pressures and inter-relationships.[133] Nizer, speaking of a judge in a case, says:

> "No doubt he was trying to be . . . impartial, but judges, like the rest of us, are affected by motivations so deep that they are hidden from their own awareness. . . . It was up to me to cast . . . doubt in his mind as well as in the jury's collective mind."

He also suggests that when a judge reserves decision on a motion to dismiss at the end of the plaintiff's case, he has "a psychological involvement in a defendant's verdict." [134]

Psychological Transactions in the Trial

The jury, by being allowed to operate within the courtroom, becomes an arm of the court, nominally bound by the rules of law. However, in its operation, the jury is actually an expression of public opinion. The court expresses the power of the state, the jury the feeling of a group of private individuals on a controversial issue. It would seem that the courts allow the jury to be a buffer between the law and the public. " 'It saves judges from the responsibility—which to many men would appear intolerably heavy and painful—of deciding simply on their own opinion upon the guilt or innocence of the prisoner.' It saved the judges of the middle ages not only from this moral responsibility, but also from enmities and feuds.

---

[132] Gair, *The Psychology of Litigation*, 20, No. 2 N.Y. COUNTY LAW. A.B. BULL. 44-49, at 48 (1962).
[133] STRYKER, THE ART OF ADVOCACY 32-34 (1954).
[134] NIZER, MY LIFE IN COURT 352 (1961).

Likewise it saved them from that as yet unattempted task, a critical dissection of testimony." [135]

Part of the great disparity between the jury and the law as vehicles of that elusive goal "justice" is that the laws that govern jury trials do not take cognizance of what we now know about many aspects of human behavior. The assumptions basic to a jury trial may be "illusory," as Judge Jerome Frank called them. This is particularly true in automobile personal injury cases where the evidence deals essentially with matters of common experience and individual perception.

In most automobile accident cases there are several eyewitnesses whose testimony will be in conflict on crucial points.[136] Judge or jury is asked to decide which side's wit-

---

[135] 2 POLLOCK & MAITLAND, THE HISTORY OF ENGLISH LAW 627 (2d ed. 1898). It has been suggested by Leifer that "The use of a 'scientific expert' to aid in the determination of responsibility eases the burden of the court by giving the impression that the determination rests on a scientifically determined fact rather than on an ambiguous matter of semantics. It thus disguises and distracts us from the fact that the courts have to justify life and death decisions on the basis of arbitrary and ambiguous criteria and provides what appears to be a scientific justification for the court's decision." Leifer, *The Psychiatrist and Tests of Criminal Responsibility* 19, 11 AMERICAN PSYCHOLOGIST 827 (1964).

[136] Examples of conflicting perceptions of witnesses which must be resolved are to be found in the 1964 *Warren Commission Report* 115, 133, 169, which analyzed the evidence concerning the assassination of President Kennedy and the murder of Patrolman Tippitt. Most of the witnesses at the scene claimed to have heard three shots. But there were some who testified hearing four and "perhaps as many as five or six shots." "Soon after the three empty cartridges were found, officials at the scene decided that three shots were fired, and that conclusion was widely circulated by the press. The eyewitness testimony may be subconsciously colored by the extensive publicity given the conclusion that three shots were fired." (*Id.* at 110-11.)

A majority of the eyewitnesses said that the three shots were not evenly spaced, most recalling the second and third shots bunched together, but there were others who thought that the first and second were. One well-placed witness recalled that the President was hit in the head by the last shot. Another, that there was a shot after the President was struck in the head. Two witnesses who testified to the bag in which Oswald was supposed to have carried the rifle estimated the size of the bag to be some six or seven inches shorter than the largest component of the rifle, and some ten inches shorter than the bag actually found. (*Id.* at 111 et seq., 133.)

Each of two sisters who positively identified Oswald in the line-up, whispering their identification to a detective, testified that she was

nesses present the more probably accurate account of the incident. They must determine whether the party having the burden of proof has achieved a preponderance of evidence. This involves a value judgment and, however well defined by the courts, it remains largely subjective. *One man's preponderance is another's failure of proof.* And there are jurisdictions in which in a case involving persons of different races it requires a preponderant preponderance for one to win and pigmentation for the other.

"Preponderance" of the evidence is a general feeling. There is no objective criterion for determining it. From a feeling about the existence of preponderance, judge or jury has to make a specific finding within the specific definition of fault liability as to whether, for example, the defendant's action was negligent and led solely and directly to the injury, an abrupt transition from art to mathematics, a process of weighing and evaluating. In view of the fact that a trial rarely can produce perceptions that are true to objective reality, and can never be complete, a court decides a case on an estimate of probability, which is an element of its expectation.[137] The jury "accepts one version as against another because it accords with its own standard of experience. The judge, when he is faced with conflicting testimony, decides on the basis of probability. We talk of the credibility of witnesses, but what we really mean is that the witness has told a story which meets the tests of plausibility and is therefore credible."[138] This is nothing more than conforming to expectations.

---

the first one to make the identification. It would appear that an ego need of each prompted a claim to first place, and for one of them distorted reality. (*Id.* at 168.)

The Commission had to pass upon a substantial number of pieces of conflicting evidence. It had the benefit of the power to examine any witness it wished. It had the assistance of the Secret Service, the F.B.I., the local police and medical and ballistic experts from all over. It was not hurried, but could take months to come to a conclusion. It did not have to act in an atmosphere of courtroom contention. No party to a litigation, civil or criminal, has this opportunity for obtaining objective evidence and no court a chance to give such meticulous consideration as the Commission did.

[137] STOGDILL, INDIVIDUAL BEHAVIOR AND GROUP ACHIEVEMENT 63 (1959).

[138] NIZER, MY LIFE IN COURT 11 (1961); see Liefer, *supra* note 135, at 828.

Between the testimony and the verdict there is still
more occasion for refraction of the original incident. At
best the reality of the case to judge and jury is a secondhand reality. With respect to the secondhand reality the
jurors' individual perceptions, interpretations, and recollections of the individual witness are subject to the same
limitations as is the witness's own story. (So too is the
judge's when he has to determine the facts where there is
no jury or perhaps on a *voir dire*.) Each juror has his own
fund of experience that will condition not only his relationship to the witnesses, but his relationship to other jurors
as well.

There are several transactions within the jury trial.
In addition to the transactions between the initial occurrence and the witness, and those between counsel and the
jury, there are those between the witness and the jury,
the judge and the jury, and among the jurors themselves.
Thus the possibility of alteration in the basic episode—the
accident itself or the breach of contract or act of adultery
or the theft—pyramids. The problem of perception of the
incident by the witness has been dealt with in Chapter I.
We can regard the witness-juror problem as similarly governed but subject to the further stress of the adversary
proceedings. What applies to a witness's observation and
the relation to reality, applies to the juror's observation
of the witness's testimony. The unreliability of memory
in witnesses is replicated to a large extent in the juryman's
memory of the evidence, especially in a case extending more
than a single day.

Inasmuch as recall is related to socio-educational status,
we can expect that judges would have better recall of the
evidence than most jurors; and they would be facilitated in
their recall by being permitted to take notes, which jurors
are not permitted to do. We could make the hypothesis also
that the more highly punitive judges and jurors would
have better recall of the evidence than the less punitive
judges and jurors. This would not mean that judges, particularly high punitive judges, would tend to reach better
conclusions than jurors. Because of their generally higher
socio-educational status we could also anticipate that judges
would make and rely on more *inferences* as well as better
recall of the evidence in making their decisions. Furthermore, it may be that, in spite of the limitations of the jury
system already discussed, group decision-making tends to

be more successful.[139] These are matters requiring considerable research before accepting the abolition of juries, even in civil suits, to speed and improve the administration of justice, in spite of the serious defects in the jury system discussed in this chapter.

We shall concentrate here on the final stage, that of the jury's deliberations. The numerous psychological factors that are brought into play at these various stages have been explored for comparable situations and are now sufficiently well understood for us to be able to apply them to the particular circumstances of litigation.

The jury's (or judge's) findings of fact are primarily conditioned by the credibility given to one witness or another. But if a juror feels more sympathy for either party, or takes a strong dislike to a witness, that emotional response will affect, if not wholly determine, the weight he gives to the evidence. A juror may not get the necessary support from the disliked or disbelieved witness to resolve a conflict in that witness's favor. If the juror feels that, in any event, the plaintiff is entitled to something simply because he was injured, he may be unable to discriminate among different degrees of accuracy represented by different stories. The keen and impartial observer, of detached Olympian judgment, is as much of a legal fiction as is the reasonable man.

We all tend to think in patterns, and thus if a witness has been a war hero, or is active in church affairs, or is a bank president, we assume not only that he is brave, or pious, or financially reliable, but also that in the entire syndrome which these traits connote, he has other admirable traits including honesty, and further, that he is telling the truth on this particular occasion. We are shocked when a bank official or a religious leader violates social standards because we have come to expect of entire classes of people greater conformity to the goals established for society than of other people. Certain stereotypes serve as our models and heroes, and we measure others by those yardsticks. Our attitudes in general are formed in relation to reference groups which we use as models.[140]

---

[139] Shaw, *Problem Solving by Individuals and Groups*, in MACCOBY, NEWCOMB & HARTLEY (eds.), READINGS IN SOCIAL PSYCHOLOGY 564, at 574-75 (3d ed. 1958).

[140] See Siegel & Siegel, *supra* note 93.

This formation of stereotypes emerges from the search for social constancy as described by Kilpatrick and Cantril.[141] It serves as the basis for our formulation of functional probabilities, just as do the patterns created by our experience on a perceptual level. But these stereotypes are, again, "essentially forms society provides in order to enable a person to get along more effectively with his own being," and are invoked to "bring greater standardizations and predictability to a wide range of behavior as well as to provide some people with common significances." So we must return to the nature of one person's judgment of another as being subjectively conditioned. It is as though each juror had a ruler by which he measured the witnesses, and each ruler was marked in fractions of inches, but they could not be standardized. The twelve can communicate in terms of inches, but not in fractions, and each fraction means something different to the next juror, and individually and as a group different to any twelve others.

When faced with something that he has previously experienced to be "bad," the juror, like the witness, will either not see it, that is, deny its existence, or reorganize his perception so that he can perceive it as bad.[142] The first, of course, is a process of psychological denial already discussed. The other is a tendency toward over-simplification as described similarly by Ross Stagner, who notes that "cues indicative of behavior contrary to our expectations are often distorted to support the rigid percepts already organized. . . . Each tends to see reality only in the manner which is compatible with his own motives and past experiences." [143] This is especially true in cases involving sex which provide the stimuli for the release of hostility which protects the ego from repressed sexual instincts.[144] Cases involving deviants and outgroups afford the opportunity

---

[141] See Kilpatrick & Cantril, *The Constancies in Social Perception*, in EXPLORATIONS IN TRANSACTIONAL PSYCHOLOGY 354-65, at 357 (Kilpatrick ed. 1961).

[142] Bronfenbrenner, *The Mirror Image in Soviet-American Relations, A Social Psychologist's Report*, 17, No. 3 J. SOCIAL ISSUES 45-56 (1961).

[143] Stagner, *Personality Dynamics and Social Conflict*, 17, No. 3 J. SOCIAL ISSUES 28, 33-34 (1961).

[144] Jones, E. & deCharms, *Changes in Social Perception as a Function of the Personal Relevance of Behavior*, in READINGS IN SOCIAL PSYCHOLOGY, *op. cit. supra* note 139, at 102.

for projection of repressed instincts and hostility in a manner which is safe.[145]

Judges and juries must be presumed to share with other mortals attitudes of aggression or withdrawal toward deviants and outgroups based on ego defensive needs, particularly where there is "encouragement . . . to its expression by some form of social support." They will also share the prejudices of the socially mobile middle class, when they are of that status [146]— which they usually are.

It is unnecessary to discuss sympathy from the point of view of empirical research or psychoanalysis. Naive psychology deriving out of the experience of each one of us makes clear that we and others are frequently motivated to act and judge out of sympathy. Most of us tend to be for "the underdog," that is, if his behavior is not threatening to our values or to our sense of social balance. Nevertheless, another legal fiction is that an emotion such as sympathy must not determine judgment. Judge and jury are expected to be objective, free from the common human trait of sympathy. This doctrine was set forth by the New York Court of Appeals in 1899 in *Laidlaw v. Sage*, where Mr. Justice Martin said:

> ". . . sympathy, although one of the noblest sentiments of our nature . . . has no proper place in the administration of the law. . . . If permitted to make it the basis of transferring the property of one party to another, great injustice would be done, the foundation of the law disturbed, and anarchy result." [147]

It would be a surprising departure to discover a lawyer who did not attempt to get judge and jury to identify with his client out of sympathy.

In the shorthand of over-simplification jurors respond to witnesses in the same manner as witnesses do to the incident itself. Each juror is himself a witness to each

---

[145] The author noticed this phenomenon on a number of occasions when the New York City Board of Education passed judgment in cases of teachers charged with improper sexual conduct.

[146] Katz, *The Functional Approach to the Study of Attitudes*, 24 PUBLIC OPINION Q. 163-80 (1960).

[147] Laidlaw v. Sage, 158 N.Y. 73 (1896). So Russell Sage was not required by judicial process to transfer any of his property to the defendant out of sympathy. It was preserved for him to transfer it to a foundation bearing his name, and to leave in perpetuity the image of one who had sympathy for the poor.

witness, perceiving and interpreting the testimony through
the lenses he has ground out of his own experience and
expectations. Prejudices toward a particular segment of
the population to which the witnesses or parties may belong
come into play here too, for many stereotypes are pegged
to particular economic, racial, ethnic, or religious groups,
and most of us are labeled in the eyes of our fellow man
by at least one of these characteristics.[148]

Where there is a lack of knowledge or perception of
some fact that we deem necessary to reach a conclusion,
this gap will tend to create in us a sense of incongruity
with respect to the remaining data. Therefore, in order to
dispel this incongruity or dissonance, we try to fill in the
gap. Because this gap results from lack of factual knowledge or perception we try to obtain further data. But the
jury cannot do this once they are in the jury room except
perhaps to have a portion of the testimony read to them.
This, however, may not meet their needs. What happens
then is what happens frequently in other situations. The
gap is filled in with rumor. Frequently this gap in knowledge creates suspicion and jurymen may create their own
rumor or even gossip. This rumor may act to justify the
feeling of hostility the jury has against one or other of
the parties or witnesses or attorneys, or it may be used
to fortify an affirmative feeling toward one of them.[149]

The trial procedure itself can shatter the juror's capacity to recall what has been said by witnesses, lawyers,
and judge. Testimony is constantly dissected and contradicted and reshaped toward partisan ends. That is the
essence of a trial; it is not a scientific or philosophical
quest for some absolute truth, but a bitter proceeding in
which evidence is cut into small pieces, distorted, analyzed,
challenged by the opposition, and reconstructed imperfectly
in summation. Even the manner in which the evidence is

---

[148] In a sense the law has fostered this outlet for prejudice, for
challenges to the credibility of witnesses were still being argued in
the 20th Century on such grounds. 3 WIGMORE, EVIDENCE § 937
(3d ed. 1940) cites a line of federal cases in which the circuit courts
actually had to rule (all held in the negative) on whether an Indian,
a Jew, or most often, a Chinese was per se an incompetent witness.
A federal rule required that white witnesses corroborate a Chinese
alien's suit for readmittance to the country (*id.* § 2066). It is therefore not surprising that these factors are considered, at least unconsciously, by many judges and jurors.

[149] FESTINGER, A THEORY OF COGNITIVE DISSONANCE 286 (1957).

initially presented affects both the witness and the juror. Careful step-by-step direct examination of one's own witness builds up a more complete, but less accurate, story than would an opening question that precipitates a narrative response which will be not only more accurate but more interesting and probably more credible to a jury. Cross-examination reportedly leads to the least complete picture of what happened.[150] Then the jury must re-create from all these fragments, interspersed with lawyers' objections, judges' rulings, and other trial procedures, the likeliest version of what happened. This version must be evaluated in the light of instructions from the bench about burdens of proof,[151] reasonable doubt, preponderance of evidence, interpretation of statutes, degrees of crime, fault liability, contributory negligence, and other matters of law.

Judge Frank believed that our entire faith in the jury system was founded on the illusion that the jurors could be expected to understand the law as expounded by the judge and also to understand their role within it: "It is inconceivable that a body of twelve ordinary men, casually gathered together for a few days, could, merely from listening to the instructions of the judge, gain the knowledge necessary to grasp the true import of the judge's words." [152] He quotes Judge Bok's observation that "juries have the disadvantage . . . of being treated like children while the testimony is going on, but then being doused with a kettleful of law . . . that would make a third-year law student blanch." [153] Judge Geller feels that a jury is deciding the verdict during the course of (especially a long, complicated) trial, and that "a charge at the end of a long trial comes too late. The sensible solution . . . is for [the judge to give]

---

[150] Marston, *Studies in Testimony*, 15 J. AMERICAN INSTITUTE OF CRIM. L. AND CRIMINOLOGY 5, 9-11 (1924).

[151] "Nevertheless, in practice, the specific rules for burden of proof make upon us the impression of vain logical verbalities,—on the whole. They are, inherently, artificial methods of controlling the mind's operations. And when applied by a judge in a form of words which the jury is supposed to put to use in the privacy of its chamber, they are unlikely to have the supposed effect,—or indeed any effect, when they are more than the simplest rules of thumb. Comparing the amount of judicial thought expended upon them, they are probably the least worthwhile part of the rules of Evidence." 1 WIGMORE, EVIDENCE § 8c, at 286 (3d ed. 1940).

[152] FRANK, J., COURTS ON TRIAL 116 (1949).

[153] *Id.* at 117.

some enlightening instructions on the law as the case goes along, with a final summarizing charge at the end." [154]

In the final stages of most trials, the transactions between the judge and jury work for their mutual protection. The heavy responsibility a juryman must carry in making a judgment ". . . based on his individual insecure intuition, is made easier in the following two ways: First, the judgment rendered is not an individual but a collective one, that of the whole jury; and second, the majorities of penal codes leave it to the learned judge, who, under the protection of the paragraphs of the law, limits their influence on the sentence and thus relieves the jury from a part of their responsibility. One can hardly be surprised to find that the attempt to protect the world of paragraphs by means of the lame intuition of the average layman is not a real way out of the crisis of our judicial system." [155]

After the evidence, the summations, and charge, the jury retires to uncomfortable quarters to deliberate. This is the phase of litigation about which we know comparatively little. The jury room is a sanctuary into which none may enter, though court factotums have been known to put ear to door. Thus what we know about how juries interact on the evidence among themselves is either deduced from the results of their deliberations, from interviews with them after judgment or from experimental, simulated situations in which persons "play jury." We can also make some assumptions based on a general knowledge of group dynamics.

Social psychologists are especially aware of the tendency toward uniformity within a group situation. The individual's own opinion is reinforced when he finds others in his group who share it.[156] A snowballing effect makes dissent increasingly difficult as the majority increases. This is especially true of matters that cannot be empirically verified, for as Muzafer Sherif found, when the validity of a hypothesis cannot be tested, its validity is likely to be de-

[154] Geller, *Experiences and Reflections of a Trial Judge*, 21 N.Y. COUNTY A.B. BULL. 118 (1963).
[155] ALEXANDER & STAUB, THE CRIMINAL, THE JUDGE AND THE PUBLIC, A PSYCHOLOGICAL ANALYSIS 41 (rev. ed. 1957). See also, Geller, *op. cit. supra* note 154, at 117.
[156] See Festinger, *Informal Social Communication*, in CARTWRIGHT & ZANDER, GROUP DYNAMICS: RESEARCH AND THEORY 286 (2d ed. 1960).

duced from the number of people who share in it. Sherif has reported that "in a situation [in which] . . . the individual is unable to tell right [from] . . . wrong, he is almost completely dependent upon the group for selecting a response." [157] The mere existence of dissent rankles, and the desire is for unanimity. Thus members of the majority, continuously addressing themselves to those in the minority, will encourage them to get on the bandwagon and thus increase the security with which the majority view can be maintained. If the determination is unchallenged, there is complete security for all who believe in it. Of course in a legal system which requires unanimity this process will be emphasized.

The forces that function to encourage uniformity include one category defined as helping the group to accomplish its purposes. A jury, to achieve its purposes, must reach a verdict, and a verdict, in most cases, requires unanimity. So here we have two overlapping pressures, one general and one specific, that will hammer out a form of agreement among the twelve jurors.

Cartwright and Zander quote Asch as describing the individual's awareness both of himself and of others in relation to the outside world: "He notes that he, as well as others, is converging upon the same object and responding to its identical properties. Joint action and mutual understanding require the relation of intelligibility and structural simplicity. In these terms the 'pull' toward the group becomes understandable," and furthermore, the momentum toward uniformity is within the individual himself, a product of his own uncertainties and need to find harmony with the world around him.[158]

For groups of twelve, it has been reported that the individual has less regard for the value of his own opinion than he does in smaller groups.[159] This is presented as a factor that reduces participation as the group increases, especially if the discussion is limited in duration. The pressure to reach a consensus tends to make the individual less de-

[157] *Introduction* to CARTWRIGHT & ZANDER, *op. cit. supra* note 156, at 165, 167, citing SHERIF, THE PSYCHOLOGY OF SOCIAL NORMS 138 (1936).

[158] *Id.* at 168.

[159] See Hare, *A Study of Interaction and Consensus in Different Sized Groups*, 17 AMERICAN SOCIOLOGICAL REV. 261, 267 (1952).

termined to maintain his position, thus producing another drive to uniformity. Applying this data, we can be certain that juries do compromise in terms of such matters as guilt, liability, and damages. This desire for harmony is evidenced not only in those cases in which the award is obviously averaged from a number of possible proposals, but also by the ways in which damages will be reduced to compensate for doubts about liability.

The University of Chicago Jury Project suggests that if the fight about liability has been heated, the jury will have exhausted its combative energies and will grasp quickly at some figure for damages. This Project's work also indicates, so far, that juries do consider many of the factors legally forbidden to them in estimating damages, clearly varying the damages awarded with the degree of negligence found, and "where facts as to liability and damages are ambiguous, damages are likely to vary with the number of dependents looking to the plaintiff for support." [160] If

---

[160] The most complete exposition of this project available to date is by Professor Harry Kalven, Jr., *Report on the Jury Project*, Univ. of Mich. Law School, CONFERENCE ON AIMS AND METHODS OF LEGAL RESEARCH (1955). He begins by noting the ambivalent role of today's jury, as evidenced by the fact that the Federal Tort Claims Act does not provide for trial by jury although the cases may be identical to those tried with a jury except that in the former instance the government is a party. (Compare workmen's compensation cases once uniformly tried by jury.)

Two separate modes of inquiry were used. One involved interviewing actual jurors selected through the courts; the other involved simulation of jury panels selected by behavioral scientists. The latter was necessary because it was not permissible for the project to hear actual deliberations in the jury room.

The work with actual juries included having an observer present throughout the trial, interviewing each juror in depth after trial to compare the first-ballot and final verdict positions. Such inquiry found that in 71% of the cases the jury was not unanimous on the first ballot, and that in 36% of the cases the division was at least 8 to 4. The project found very few instances in which the minority view ultimately prevailed, that where the original minority was only one or two it was always overwhelmed, and that hung juries occurred only when there was a substantial minority, that is, where the dissenters found substantial support.

This can be explained by the fact that one who deviates from the group goal, in this case reaching a verdict, will feel more rejection by the other members of the group than where the deviation is irrelevant to the group's goal. Schachter, *Deviation, Rejection and Communication*, 46 J. ABNORMAL PSYCHOLOGY 190-207 (1951).

this be so, then we can conclude that the law with which the judge charges the jury is another "As If" situation, another legal fiction.

Judges, where they sit without juries, will probably form their judgments in a similar manner. This is an appropriate subject for research before we abolish juries even in civil cases.

The Project's studies also indicate that juries do consider taxability of the award, attorney's fees, interest, and insurance, even though they are not supposed to do so. In one sample case tried before three experimental juries, when the matter of insurance was raised casually at the trial, and was not contested by the defendant's lawyer, the damages awarded were considerably lower than when counsel objected, the objection was sustained, and the judge instructed the jury to disregard what they had just heard. This legalistic byplay had more firmly entrenched in the jurors' minds the question of insurance, so that even though it was raised in a negative context, it was a prominent and formative consideration. The verdict when the insurance matter was raised and ignored was only slightly higher than when it was not raised at all, indicating perhaps that the average defendant in a negligence suit is assumed to be insured, and only when this becomes a major issue does the existence of insurance greatly affect the verdict.

The Jury Project was also interested in attitudes toward jury service both before and after participation. The major result here was "generally an affirmative response to jury service" but with major objections to the waste of time and the economic loss that such service entailed.

The Experimental Jury Project technique involved recordings of mock trials that were based on actual trials. The same tapes were played to different juries, or sometimes one element of the trial was changed to measure the impact of that element on the jury. The deliberations of these juries have been recorded, with the full knowledge of the participants. The jurors have also been interviewed before the completion of the trial. They were questioned before the deliberations began, and afterwards, and asked to describe their change of mind, if one occurred. Three moot cases have been developed thus far and played to over 50 moot juries. The project reports that jurors seem to get totally involved in their deliberations and give them full attention. Juries have hung, and have deliberated at great length. The three cases used deal with an automobile accident injury, an insanity defense comparing the effects of the *M'Naghten* and *Durham* rules, and a products liability suit. This project has also done some work on comparing the verdicts that jurors reach with those of judges in the same case, and have found that the two correlate more closely than expected.

As every lawyer knows, the idea that a party carries
insurance need not be crudely presented during the trial.
It can be more subtly implanted in the *voir dire* of prospective jurors. So can other biases inadmissible, or perhaps
unprovable, at the trial be suggested on the *voir dire*.[160a]
The case then proceeds to verdict and judgment on the fiction that it is determined on the evidence, As If the biasing
on the *voir dire* had never occurred.

Judge Charles Clark, commenting on the Project's report, said that "The jury is too fine, as well as too clumsy
and expensive an instrument for all this load (referring
especially to the Southern District of New York), . . . it
just isn't the correct way to achieve sound policy for the
victims of this industrial age and our modern civilization."

There has been much debate as to the value of juries.
We need not here enter this controversy. Certainly the area
in which the law permits juries to act is severely circum-
scribed by the judicial charge and the rules of evidence.
"Based as they are upon the principles of inductive logic,
the philosophy behind them is that laymen are not logicians
and therefore should be prevented from hearing facts from
which illogical conclusions are irresistible." [161]

Laymen may not be good logicians. Can they, then, be immune from drawing the illogical conclusions from the evidence of witnesses? Fault liability, the area that contributes
the largest number of cases to our congested courts, relies
almost entirely on the observations of eyewitnesses or on
witnesses who may hear, illusory and unreliable as such
testimony may be. Whether their conclusions, based on
their premises, are logical or not, their premises are in
large measure founded on unreality or derived from the
reality of witnesses whose perceptions are in conflict.

It is the principle of fault liability that governs most
personal injury litigation. Our present method of handling
negligence claims is a costly way *not* to accomplish our
purpose.[162] The purpose, presumably, is to determine those
at fault and compel them to compensate those they have
injured; but ". . . road accidents do not usually have a single
'cause' " and "each individual accident is likely to have

[160a] See KAPLAN & WALTZ, THE TRIAL OF JACK RUBY 91-92 (1965).
[161] STRYKER, *op. cit. supra* note 133, at 35.
[162] Marshall, *The Unreality of Accident Litigation: A Plea for
a New Approach*, 50, No. 8 A.B.A.J. 713-18 (1964).

several causative factors. . . . The search for single causes
of accidents is usually likely to prove unproductive." [163]
Where, we may ask, is the logic of searching for a nonexistent single cause by taking testimony of misperceptions
inaccurately and selectively recalled?

Fault liability is based on fictions. It is these fictions,
these As Ifs, that clog our court calendars, not a paucity
of judges or calendar practices or pretrial procedures.

Dean Wigmore concluded years ago that within the
arena of adversary proceedings little will be gained by
making better rules.

> "Our *judges* and our *practitioners* must *improve in
> spirit* as a prerequisite for any hope of real gain to
> be got from better rules. In the end, the man is more
> important than the rule. Better rules will avail little,
> if the spirit of using them does not also improve.

> "Counsel must become less viciously contentious, more
> skillful, more intent on substance than on skirmishing
> for a position." [164]

Wigmore himself apparently believed such a change is
unlikely.

> ". . . to *abolish* the bulk of the rules *now*, in the ordi-
> nary courts, would be a *futile* attempt. To pass a law
> (supposing this possible, in the hasty manner of
> of our legislation) would amount to little or nothing.
> You cannot by fiat legislate away the brain-coils of
> one hundred thousand lawyers and judges; nor the
> traditions embedded in a hundred thousand recorded
> decisions and statutes. And the plain fact is that
> trials are today being managed by these men and
> these books, as the living receptacle of the rules." [165]

What is required is social invention in the law based
on findings of the social sciences. As the statements of
lawyers already quoted indicate, many of these findings
are no surprise to them. But in their operational world
they tend to deny the existence of such realities and to
focus on the "As Ifs," their legal fictions. This is the

---

[163] Norman, *Road Traffic Accidents*, 11, No. 12 WORLD HEALTH
ORGANIZATION PAPER 19 (1962).

[164] 1 WIGMORE, *op. cit. supra* note 151, at 263.

[165] *Id.* at 259-60.

lawyer's way of resisting change, of resolving the incon-
gruities between the law and reality.

If, as Dean Wigmore says, it would be futile to attempt
to abolish the bulk of our rules—and presumably to adopt
new ones that are more realistic—could we not as first steps
withdraw from the area of fiction those legal processes
which most offend reality and for which acceptable substi-
tutes can be found? Could we not search for ways, wherever practicable, to solve by other methods conflicts now
submitted to trial?

CONCLUSION

In a civilization so largely founded on scientific method, and in which daily living is so dependent upon the application of scientific findings, the theory and practice of law remain largely immune to this prevailing cultural pattern. Though science appears in the courtroom at times in the form of evidence, and tests derived from the natural sciences are used in specific cases, those findings of the psychological sciences which apply directly to and challenge the precepts and practices of our courts are largely ignored. It is as though lawyers and judges indulged in the psychological process of denial which has been discussed in connection with witnesses. The law as we practice it is a backwash from the theory of "natural law," which is blocked from contact with the otherwise empirical nature of our culture. "Right" and "wrong" still seem to have a theological connotation of "good" and "bad" more than a scientific one of relativity, situation or predictability.

The conservatism of lawyers is supported by their intellectual and economic vested interest in traditional concepts and behavior which, as with other people, are threatened by change. The common attitude of the bar and political scientists is that knowing these defects in our trial system, the system nevertheless serves a purpose, and is certainly better than the more primitive systems from which it grew. It does not help to make an issue of the assumptions on which our laws of evidence are based. Why disturb the *Als Ob* of the courtroom? Will this not bring the law into contempt?

Of course, our legal procedures as they exist serve social purposes. But it is when they lack validity or reality that the laws will tend to be held in contempt. It should be apparent that our courts are not giving satisfaction today when we see how large a proportion of commercial cases are submitted to arbitration or settled out of court and what a large proportion of negligence cases never reach the courtroom.

Above all, what is indicated is establishment of a closer relationship between law and psychology, and participation by lawyers and psychologists in empirical research into the processes of the law. This is practically non-

103

existent, and it is curious in view of the common deductive approach of both science and law. In the law, however, there is unwillingness to experiment — sometimes for good reasons, dealing as it does with life in the living — but principally, one suspects, because lawyers have intellectual and emotional investment in the fictions of the As If.

Science demands precision but not certainty. Law aims at certainty but lacks precision because its quest for certainty glosses over the innumerable variables of individual and situational diversities, which probably will always cause law to be uncertain. Nevertheless, lawyers tend to dispose of variables and diversities by rationalization and by attempting to fit the individual *man* into a legal formula for *men*. To assume a scientific approach and seek precision amidst uncertainty would mean accepting uncertainty; and this would upset the balance of lawyers and appear to threaten the stability and the "majesty of the law." There must still be fought in the realm of law the struggles that philosophy and theology had to go through when confronted by the natural sciences.

This is not the first time that science and legal process have been in conflict. Heretics and witches, or better witches and other heretics (for after the 12th Century witches were deemed heretics in most parts of the western world) were tried by methods which today appear horrible and absurd. The *auto-da-fé*, ordeals by fire, hot irons or water as well as oral examinations were the accepted method of inquiry until the 18th Century. Kangaroo courts and lynchings were not uncommon. One of the most ingenious guilt-determining methods of the law was a flotation process in which the opposite thumbs and big toes of the girls were tied together before they were thrown into the water to sink or float. In 1489 the art of the Inquisitors became codified in the *Malleus Maleficarum* or Inquisitor's Manual, "from which they plied their tortured victims with questions and were able to extract such confessions as they desired; by a strange perversion these admissions, wrung from their victims by rack or thumbscrew, were described as voluntary." [166]

In the 16th Century some doubts as to the prevalence of witches and the methods of their prosecution arose. John Wier (or Weyer) wrote two books on the subject

---

[166] *Witchcraft*, 28 ENCYCLOPAEDIA BRITANNICA 757 (11th ed. 1911).

which became popular. He was a physician who studied
witches, "unmasking the cheaters and the charlatans,"
and concluded that witches were in fact only mentally de-
ranged old women and not heretics at all. He called for
an end to their torture and execution. The more con-
servative legal minds of the day who had their intellectual
and emotional commitment to the existing methods, that
is, the inquisitors and theologians, attacked him and his
supporters. Did not the authority of Thomas Aquinas,
several popes and ecclesiastical synods support the existence of witchcraft? It was said that thanks to Wier
and his followers "the affairs of the Devil were brilliantly
progressing." [167]

In the 17th Century, with the establishment of The
Royal Society in England, "the whole force of the English
intellect was directed to the study of natural phenomena,
and to the discovery of natural laws." This resulted in
a "general disposition to attribute to every event a natural
cause." There followed the conviction that to attribute
phenomena to witches was absurd. Nevertheless, in 1664,
Sir Matthew Hale, in sentencing two women to be hung
as witches, stated that "the reality of witchcraft was un-
questionable; 'for first, the Scriptures had affirmed so
much; and secondly, the wisdom of all nations had provided laws against such persons, which is an argument of
their confidence of such a crime.' " [168]

Here science and law were squarely in opposition. This
is a dramatic example of the law declaring "the truth of
a proposition" because it is the law. Such logic is, of course,
anathema to science but not unknown to law in other instances. Fortunately, science won out, and with the aban-
donment of the inquisition of witches, witches themselves
disappeared. People no longer looked at phenomena with
the expectation of finding witchcraft but with the expectation of finding natural causes.

Trial by battle had its day, too — a long day beginning
in primitive societies. Well into the 15th Century, before
the laws of evidence which we know today were used, a
litigant had the right to choose between witnesses — who
in fact merely took an oath to the righteousness of the litigant's case — or subjecting himself to an ordeal by com-

---

[167] CASTIGLIONI, ADVENTURES OF THE MIND 253 (1946).
[168] LECKY, HISTORY OF THE RISE AND INFLUENCE OF THE SPIRIT OF
RATIONALISM IN EUROPE (1914).

bat, either in person or through a substitute. But when the "glorious" days of chivalry passed, the powerful arm or the skilled use of weapons (the contestants perhaps wearing the favors of more or less fair ladies) were superseded by judges and juries as a means to determine the truth of the cause. The vestigial remains of trial by battle were trial in a courtroom and dueling. Dueling itself is an example of the confusion by the parties between a search for *justice* and *justification*, which is still an element in litigation.

For how many litigants want *justice* if it does not appear to them to be *justification* evidenced by a judgment, an injunction, or dismissal of the complaint or charge?[169] Certainly this search for justification is a psychological need which ought not to be dismissed lightly or cynically. The question for us, however, is whether it serves society to satisfy such a need in a spirit of contentiousness and the assumption of the law that people hear, see and recall what has occurred without relation to their previous experiences and their expectations. We have noted that this produces testimonial results that contradict or distort reality. Is it to the interest of society, to the interest of a respected judicial system to justify such procedures, as Judge Hale did witchcraft, in reliance upon common practice?

The courtroom has its realities for lawyers, judges, juries, factotums and taxpayers. It also has realities for witnesses and parties — sometimes the grim realities of the punitive aspect of much of the law. But the material with which the court works, the grain or grist to the mill of justice, is a fantasy world of "make-believe" assumptions of As Ifs, as Cardozo referred to them.

It is a Kafkaesque world in which people testify to what they neither saw nor heard accurately, nor recalled nor communicated fully, and in which victory was an end in itself, and men and women compromised to reach a decision which they based upon partially understood testimony, partisan arguments and abstract judicial charges. Life and liberty, property and reputation are staked on bets or guesses as to what really happened.

There is need for joint research by lawyers and social scientists as to the reliability of evidence which depends upon observation and recollection. Such research should

---

[169] See ch. III *supra*, and for special reference to police, see Toch, *Psychological Consequences of the Police Role, supra* note 127.

also attempt to answer the question: What possible techniques can be used to avoid the distortions now prevalent in testimony? [170] Effort should be made to reconcile the rules of evidence and conduct of trials with what we know about the nature of perception. Granted we do not know nearly all there is to know concerning perception; lack of knowledge concerning motor fuels did not bar the invention and use of combustion engines, nor, unfortunately, did incomplete knowledge of the atom block our splitting it over Hiroshima.

---

[170] An example of how courts can modify their procedure on the basis of empirical research in which the court participates is the change in the rules relating to pretrial conferences in New Jersey. Questions had been raised as to the effectiveness of the pretrial conferences and the Supreme Court decided to postpone final decision until it had data from a controlled experiment. The results of this experiment are described in Rosenberg, The Pretrial Conference and Effective Justice (1964) and were used as the basis for pretrial procedural reform. Delmar, *The Pretrial Conference and Effective Justice — A Review*, 20, No. 5 The Record of the Association of the Bar of the City of New York 288-93 (May 1965).

APPENDIX

SUGGESTED PROJECTS FOR RESEARCH AND DISCUSSION BY LAWYERS AND SOCIAL SCIENTISTS JOINTLY

1. (a) We know that in all perception and recall there is a selective process which limits the number of items in any field (in any happening) which are perceived and recalled. Does this selective process differ among different socio-educational groups and subcultures of a nation, and if so, how?

(b) Is the selective process different for witnesses, judges and jurors?

(c) Does the selective process differ between participants in a happening and witnesses to it?

2. The adversary nature of the trial procedure puts pressure on witnesses and tends to bias them in favor or against the parties. (a) What is the nature of these pressures and biases and how do they affect recall?

(b) What are the effects of examination and cross-examination (and different styles of examination and cross-examination) on witnesses? The same questions can be asked as to judges and jurors.

(c) Do these effects of direct and cross-examination differ with relation to witnesses who have previously been on the witness stand and those who appear for the first time?

(d) Does the nature of the case make a difference (commercial cases, accident cases, criminal trials, insanity trials)?

3. Witnesses who are not parties to a litigation may be called because they are otherwise involved (as member of family, employee of a party, official of bank or government), or because they have seen or heard the happening which is the subject of the litigation and volunteer to

testify, or because they have seen or heard the happening and been subpoenaed. To what extent do they identify with (support consciously or unconsciously) the side for which they are called to testify? Does it make a difference whether they are witness-participants or otherwise involved in the happening, voluntary or involuntary witnesses?

4. Does prior writing of recall reinforce the accuracy or inaccuracy of recall later testified to orally?

5. We have evidence that police tend to be more punitive than some other groups of the population. There is also evidence that experience in the role of policeman tends to produce characteristic responses to ambiguous situations resulting in the perception of more violence and greater suspiciousness than in other population groups and that the tendency grows stronger the longer one is on the force. To what extent is this greater punitiveness the result of a self-selection process by people seeking police careers, a selective process by those who recruit or choose police-men, or a process of adaptation to the role, the career of policeman, or all three?

6. If high-punitive and low-punitive people recall differently, (a) to what extent will they make more or less reliable witnesses or better jurors?

(b) Is there a difference in the way in which high-punitive and low-punitive witnesses, judges and juries adapt to the adversary conditions of the trial?

7. In order to minimize the effects on recall of the "adversary duel" in the courtroom, (a) how could trial practices be modified?

(b) What changes in trial practices might produce greater objectivity in testimony? (For example, a comparative study might be made of the Anglo-American and continental systems of presentation of evidence and their relative effects on judge and jury.)

(c) What legal procedures could be withdrawn from the courtroom and handled in a different manner in the interest of effective justice (for example, withdrawing motor vehicle accidents from the courts and adopting procedures similar to those in workmen's compensation cases)?

8. What are the effects of judicial charges on the deliberations and determinations of juries, *i.e.,* to what extent are juries influenced by judicial charges in different kinds of cases?

9. Finally, (a) are juries and judges prejudiced on a *voir dire* (the preliminary inquiry into the acceptability of an individual as a juror in a particular case, or the preliminary inquiry by a judge as to the admissibility of a piece of evidence such as a confession, etc., or into the competence of a witness)?

(b) What procedures might be instituted to meet the purposes of the *voir dire* that would minimize its prejudicing effects? (For example, does the examination of prospective jurors by judges produce less bias than that done by attorneys? Would it be less biasing if a judge other than one conducting the trial were to preside at a *voir dire* hearing?)

INDEX

Adler, Mortimer, 3
Ames, A., Jr., 18
Aquinas, Thomas, 104
Articulation
  communication, 9
  defined, 9
  distortion
    clarity of image, 37
    gaps in narrative, 37
  inferences, 37
  jury, 9
  language
    accent, 38
    pronunciation, 38
    rigidifying process, 37
    uses, 38
  witnesses, 9
Asch, Solomon E., 97
As If (Make-Believe, Fictions),
  7, 8, 83, 85, 99, 100, 101, 103,
  104, 106
Automobile Accidents
  causative factors, 101
  perception
    distance, 16
    motion, 16
  personal injury cases, 100
  speed, 18
  velocity, 18
  weight, 18
  witnesses
    bias, 18
    conflicting testimony, 18,
    88
Bias
  automobile accident cases, 18
  insanity, 66
  voir dire, 100
Bok, Curtis, 95
Browning, Robert, 53
Burden of Proof
  See EVIDENCE
Cantril, Hadley, 24, 37, 52, 92
Cardozo, Benjamin, 7, 106
Carroll, Lewis, 27

Cartwright, Dorwin, 97
Clark, Charles, 100
Communication
  See ARTICULATION
Consistency, 23, 35, 92
Contributory Negligence
  instructions, 95
Criminal Cases
  accomplices, 35
  attorneys
    consistent witnesses, 35
  co-conspirators, 35
  confessions, 38
  police lineup, 35
  punishment, 70, 78
  weight, 18
  witness for prosecution, 35
Criminal Law
  degrees of crime, 95
  punishment, 70, 78
  reasonable doubt, 95
  sentencing, 96
Damages
  dependents of plaintiff, 98
  instructions, 99
  insurance, 99
  negligence, degree, 98
Denial, Psychological, 33, 84
Dissonance, Cognitive, 33, 84, 85,
  94
Edman, Irwin, 38
Eliot, George, 2
Estes, Billy Sol, 6
Evidence
  burden of proof, 89
  changes in rules of, 101
  conclusions, 38
  confessions, 38
  declarations against interest,
    38
  evaluation
    judge, 83
    jury, 83
  hearsay rule, 14
  make-believe, 8

113